EASY PIANO
CHRISTMAS MELODIES
FOR KIDS
AND BEGINNERS

Famous melodies
in order of difficulty
with fingerings
and note names

Janis Watson

☞ <u>SCAN HERE TO ACCESS</u>
<u>THE VIDEO TUTORIALS</u>

OR ACCESS THE FOLLOWING LINK:
https://urly.it/3zjc4

<u>50 VIDEO TUTORIALS</u>
A Unique Learning Experience

1 The video tutorials **are specifically designed for children and adults** who are approaching the study of the piano for the first time.

2 The video tutorial **is an extremely useful tool that can help you play the piano with ease and immediacy**. In addition to learning the basics, you can have fun playing famous pieces right from the beginning.

3 The dual keyboard allows for better visualization of notes with illuminated keys on one keyboard **and the other keyboard helps understand which finger to use to press the key.**

4 The video tutorials **are exclusive to those who have purchased the book.**

I start by saying that each phase of learning does not need so many elements but the necessary elements at its level

I said this because I see many other books that insert as many elements as possible to try to convince them to buy their book, but the reality is that too many concepts can confuse the student and therefore not not get the results promised by the book

The book is aimed at those who start from scratch both in practice and in theory (child, teenager or adult), the book is structured in such a way as to be able to gradually learn both music and the piano, without theoretical notions (or an explanation of musical notions), precisely because at this level I do not consider them necessary

In fact, you just need to know these few things:
- the numbers written above or below the notes (see image) indicate the fingers of the hands, as indicated by the image of the two hands
- what you need to know is that notes written in treble clef (see image) should be played with the right hand, while notes written in bass clef (see image) should be played with the left hand at this point you just have to press the key indicated by the number (see images)

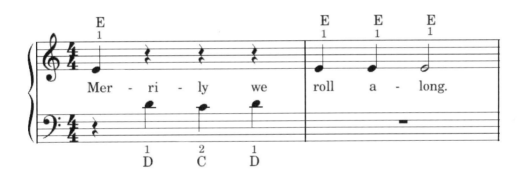

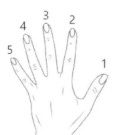

Left hand

Right hand

Bass Clef

Treble Clef

- To know where to play the notes written on the piano staff, just look at the image below:

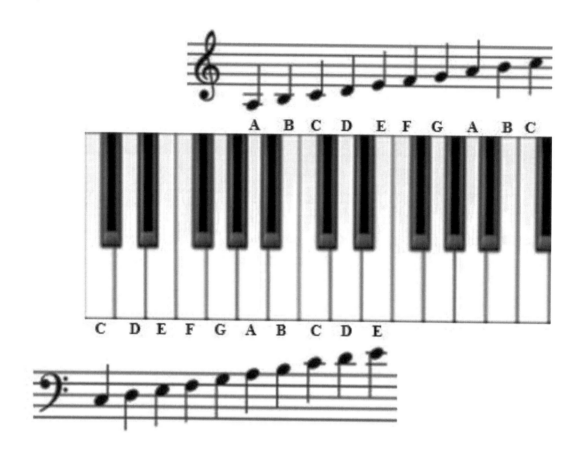

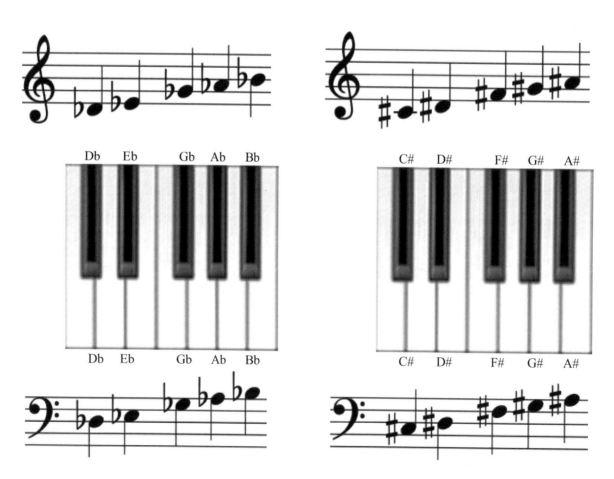

I did not add information on the rhythm precisely because **I find it more effective to understand the tempo by listening to the piece in the first phase of learning** (see link or QrCode), on the contrary, adding **too many notions in this respect leads to a confused performance** , whereas for those with minimal rhythmic notions can read the piece directly from the score

If you wish **, you can play the songs even just by watching the video tutorials thanks to the dual keyboard** , to see which key to press look at the keyboard with the lit keys, while to see which finger to use look at the keyboard with your hands (see picture):

Tips for studying songs:
- first listen to the song
- study and memorize the melody on the keyboard, using the methods indicated above
- play the piece focusing on the interpretation or just the music

I believe that in this initial phase of learning, it is more important and more effective to work on listening to the piece and playing it on the piano, as explained by the latest theories on learning music.
I suggest you to deepen the theory only later

Have fun and good music

INDEX

Jingle Bells

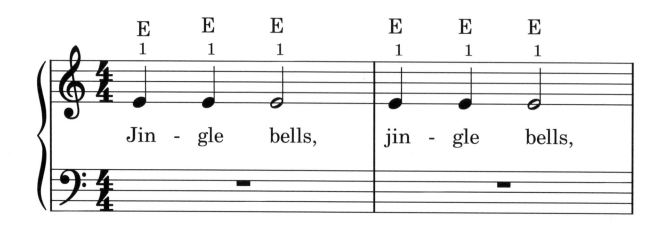

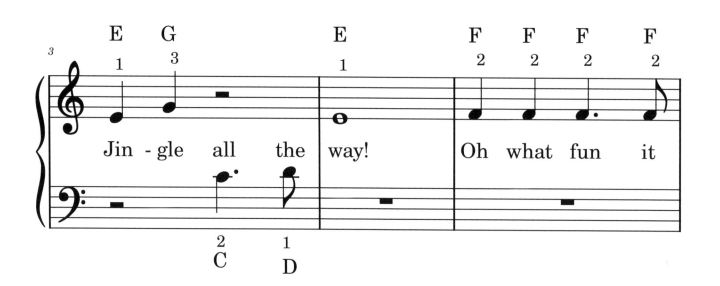

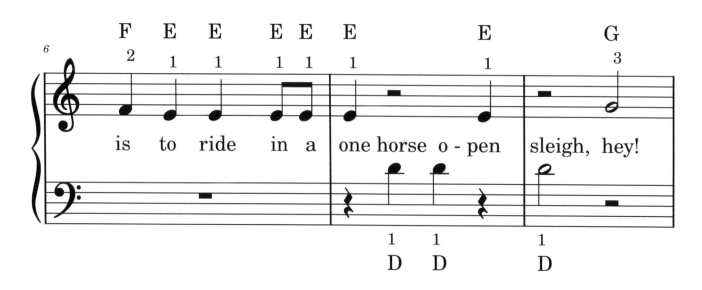

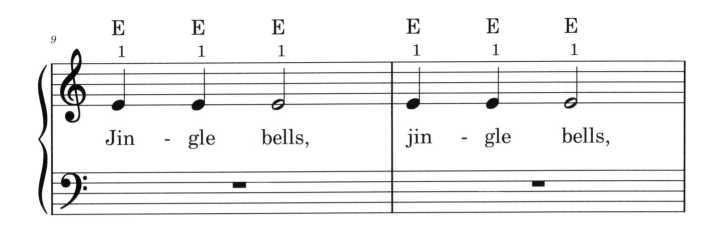

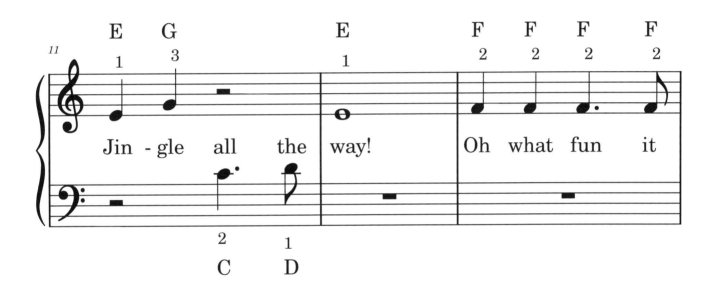

Deck the Hall

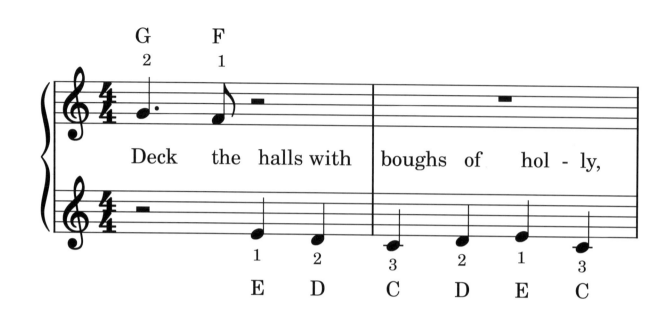

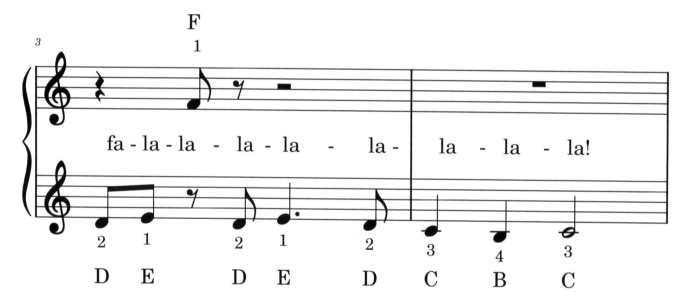

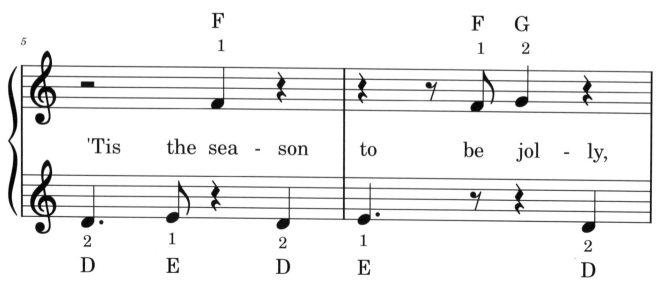

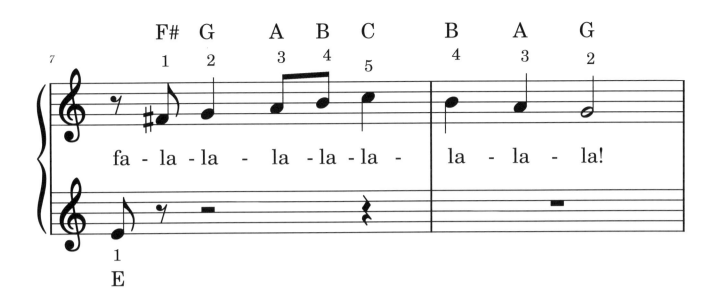

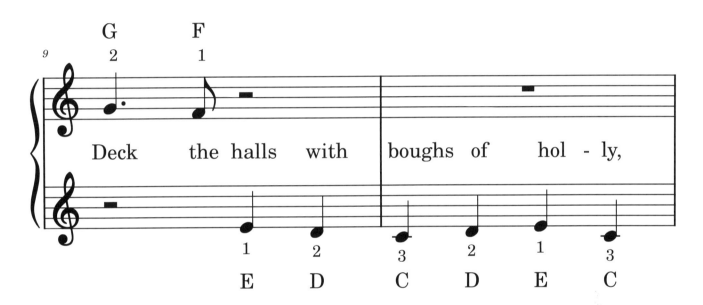

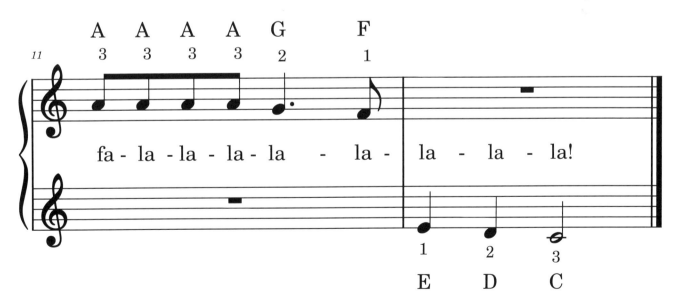

Silent Night

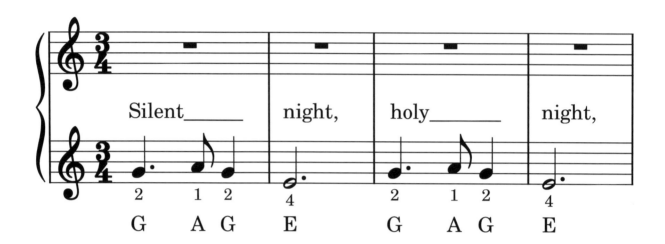

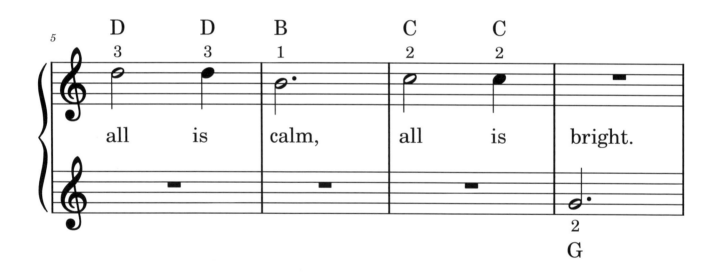

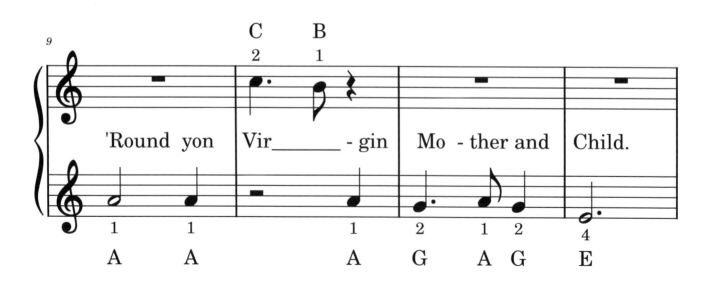

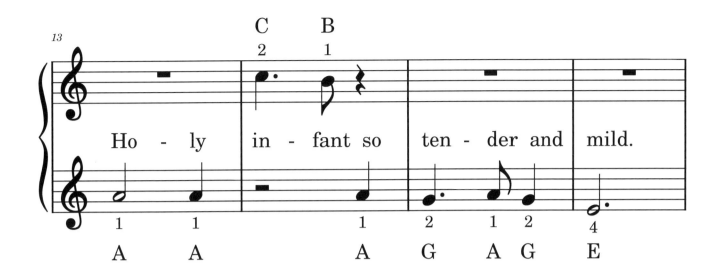

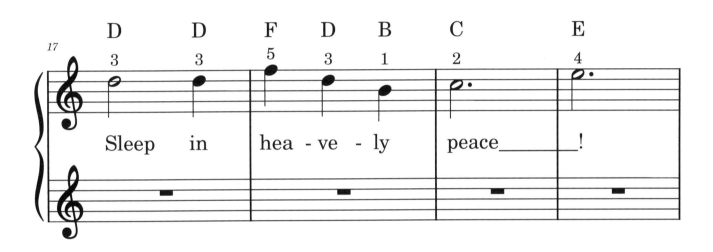

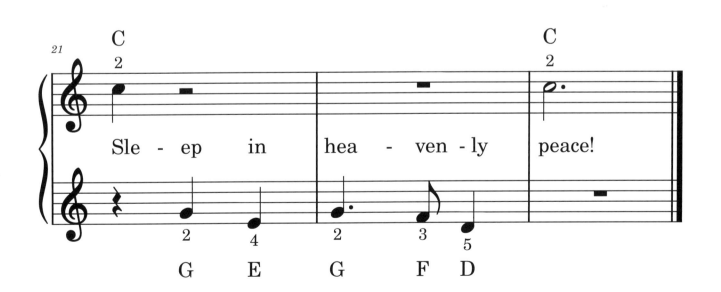

Oh Christmas Tree

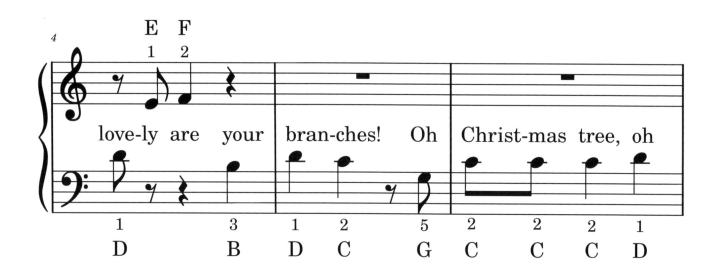

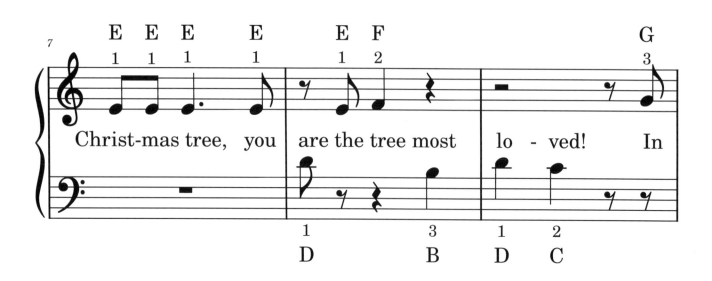

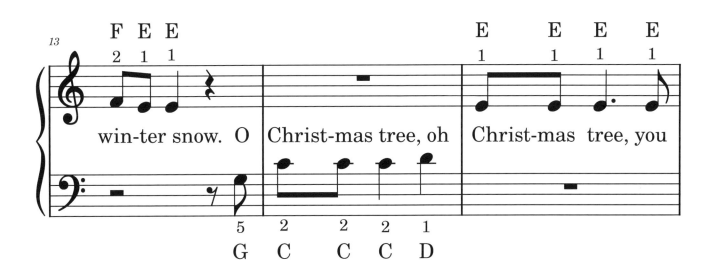

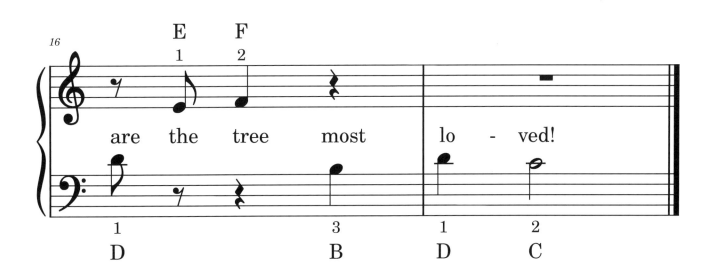

We Wish You a Merry Christmas

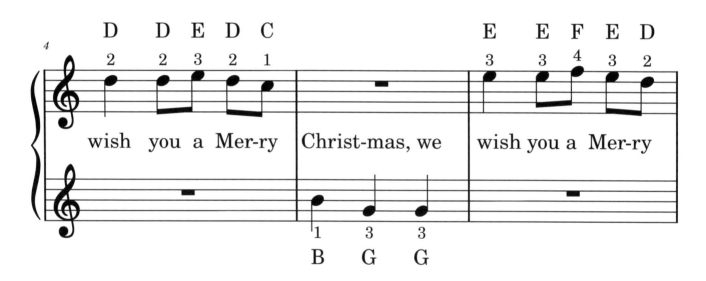

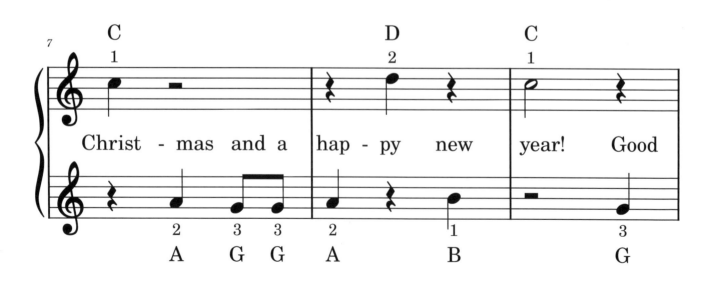

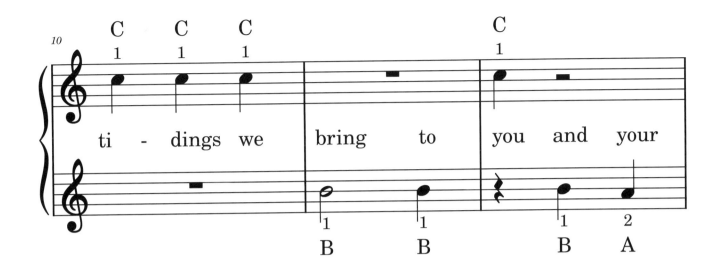

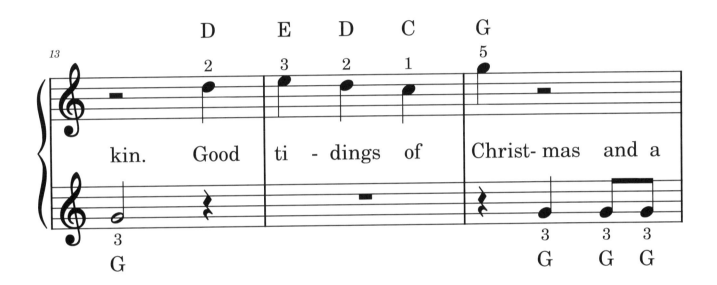

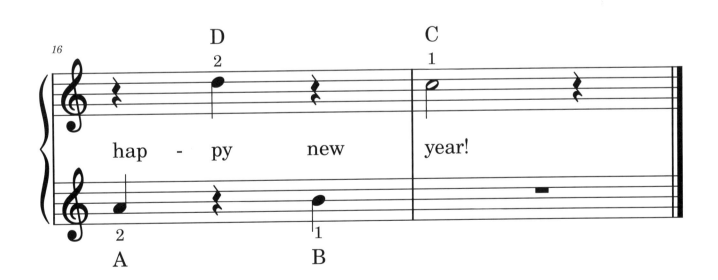

Oh Come All Ye Faithful

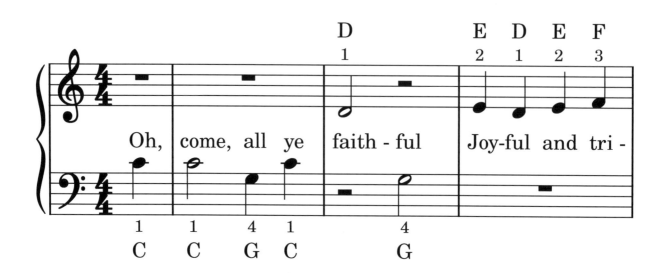

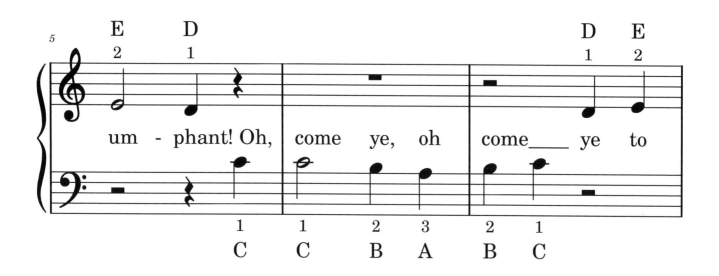

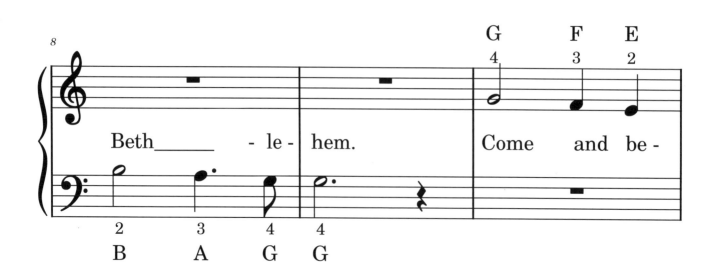

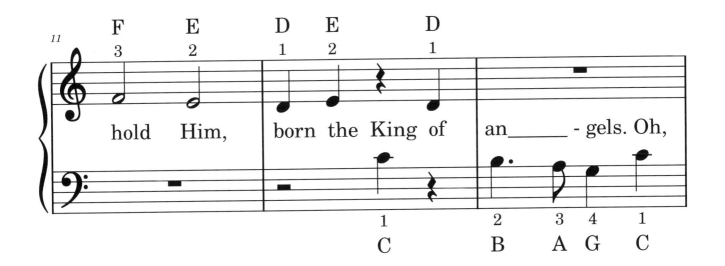

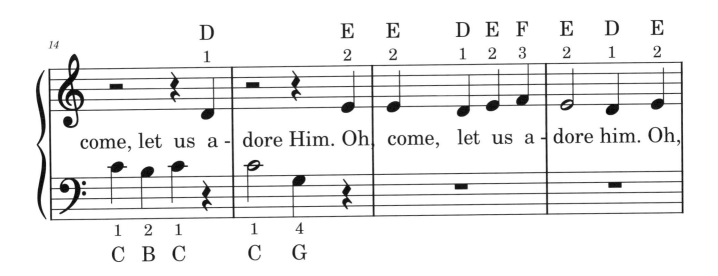

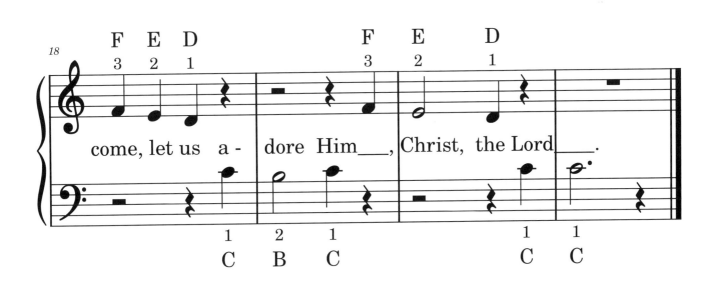

The First Noel

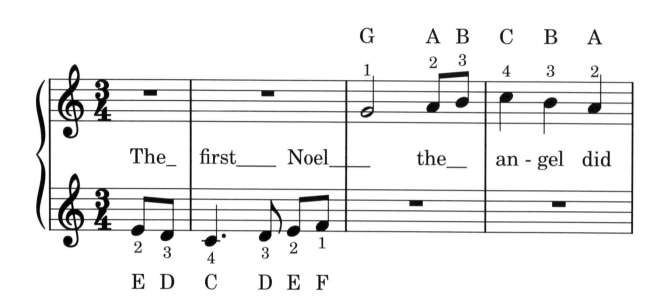

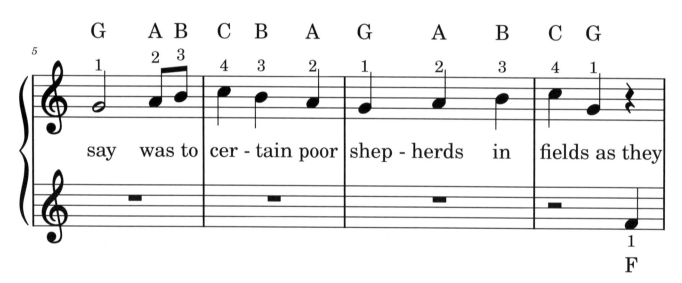

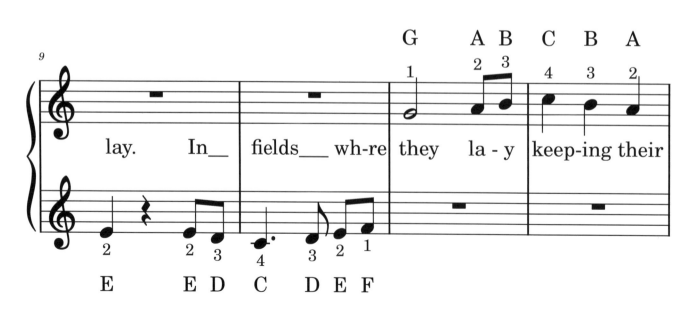

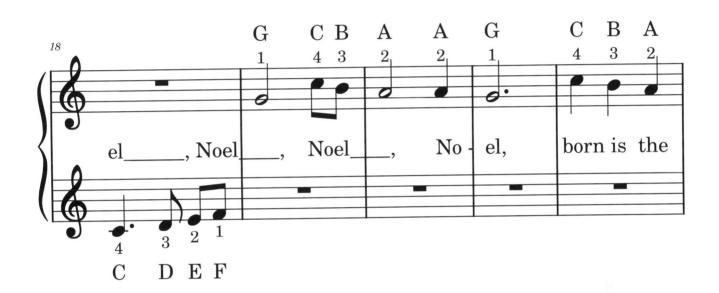

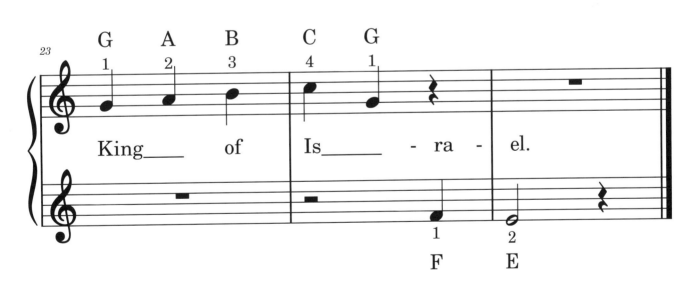

Joy to the World

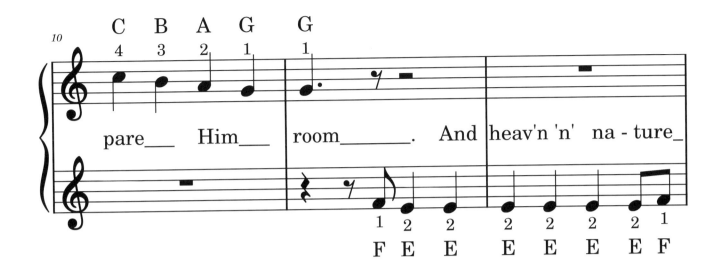

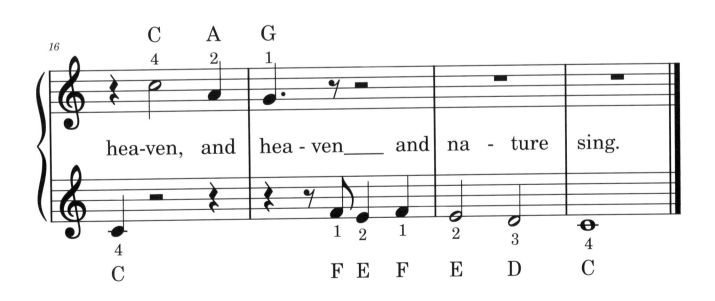

Auld Lang Syne

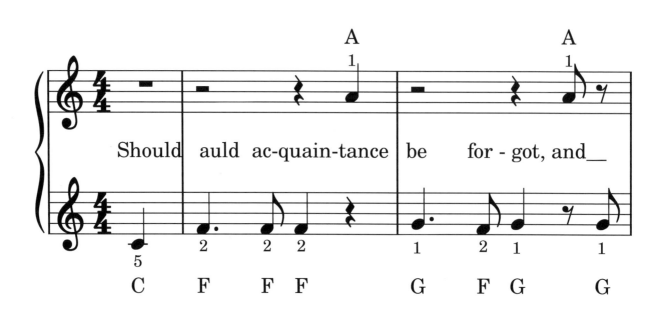

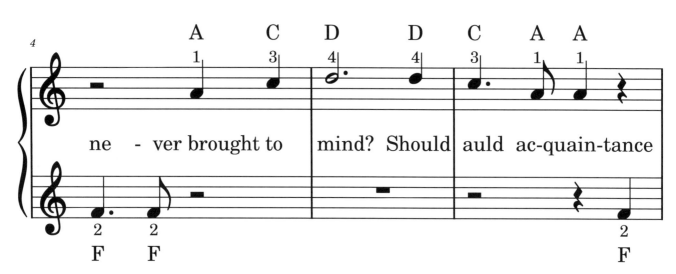

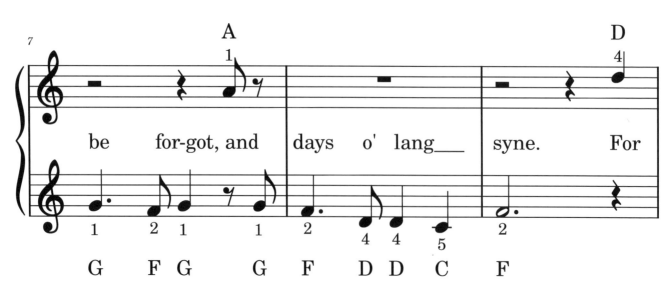

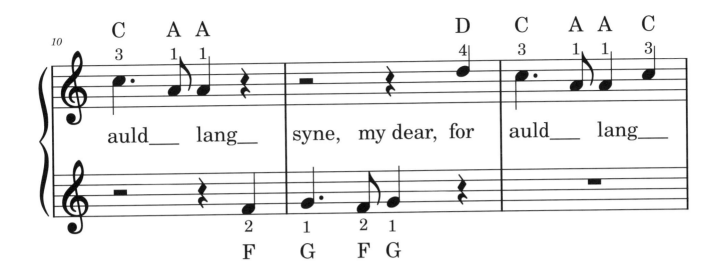

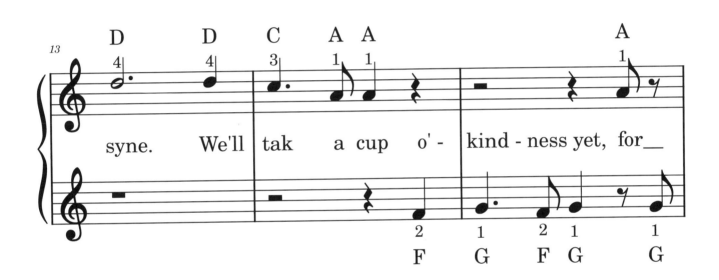

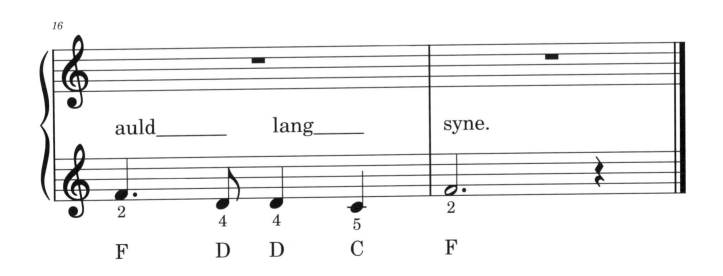

I Saw Three Ships

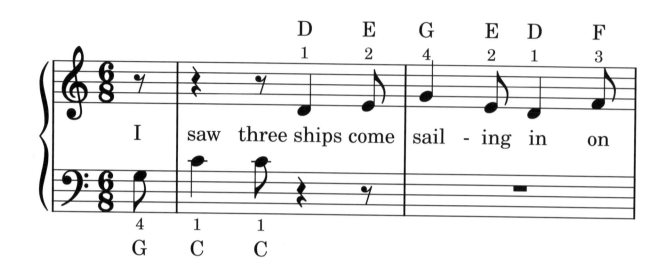

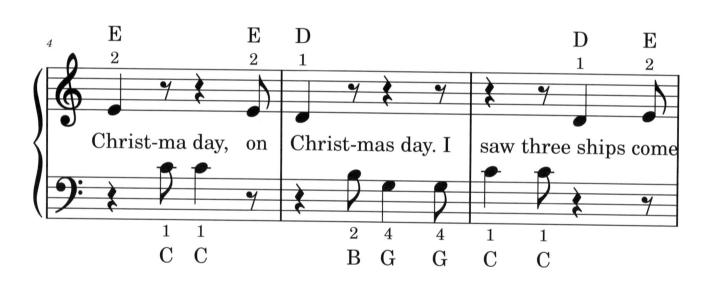

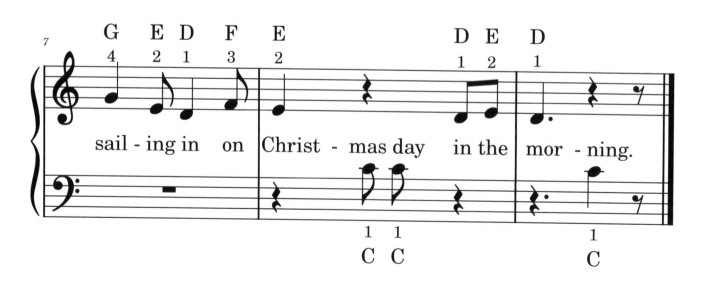

Oh Holy Night

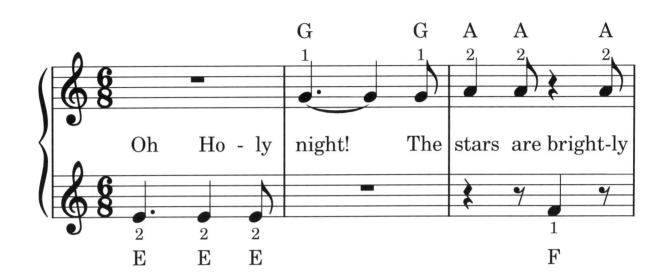

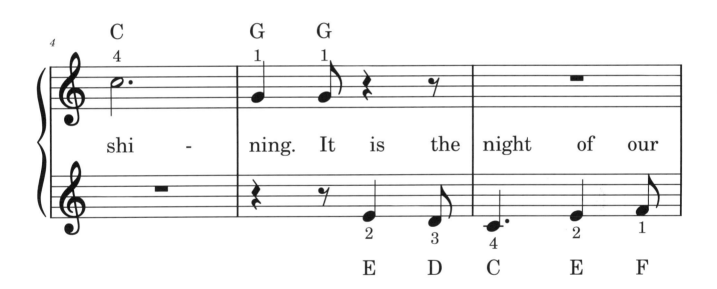

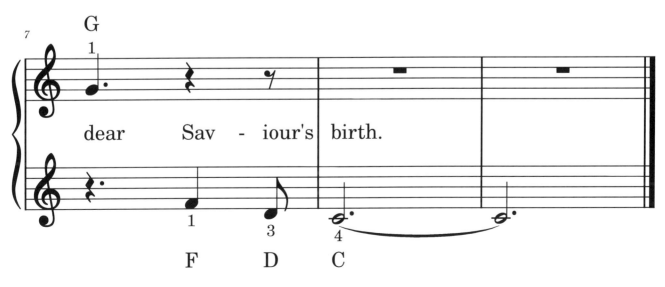

O Little Town of Bethlehem

Angels We Have Heard on High

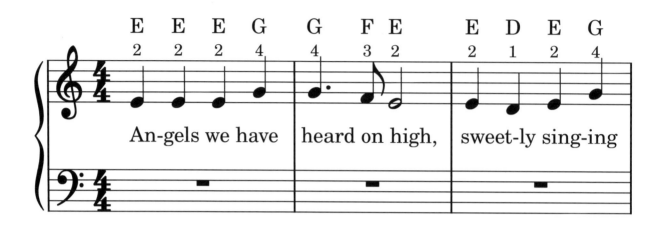

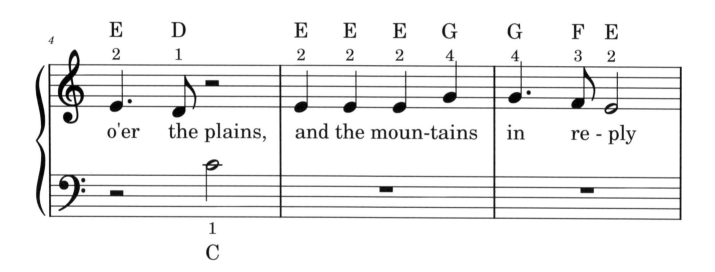

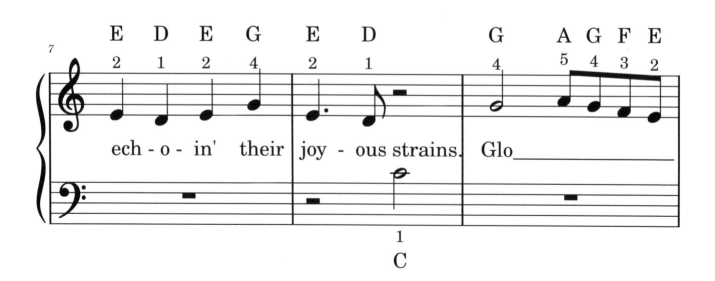

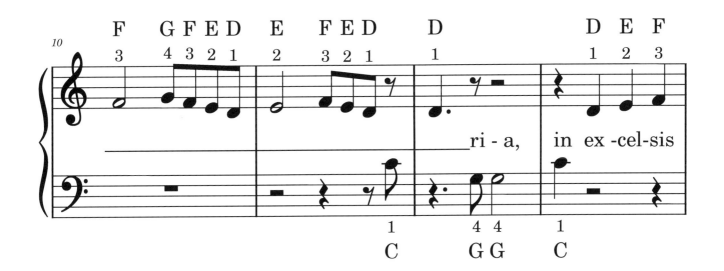

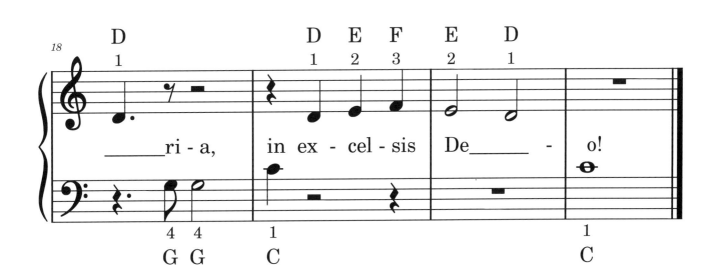

31

Hark! The Herald Angels Sing

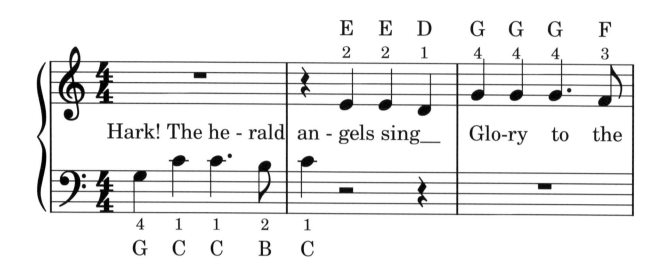

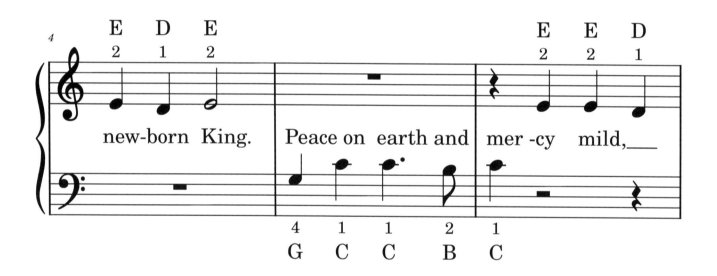

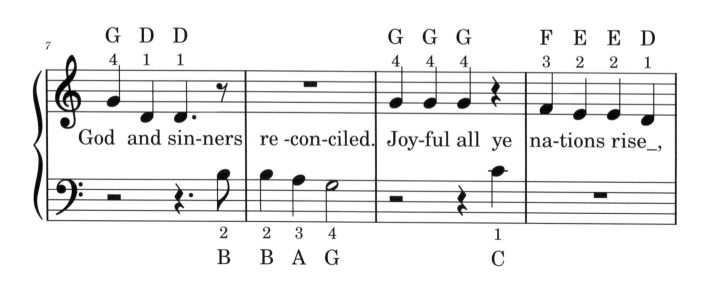

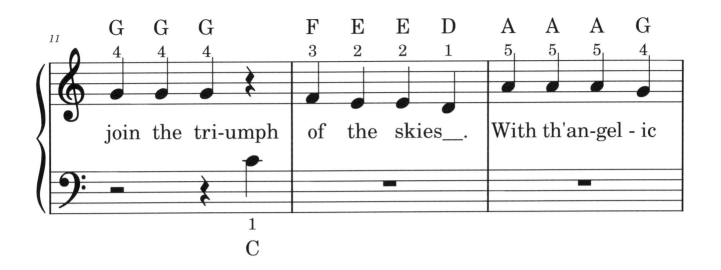

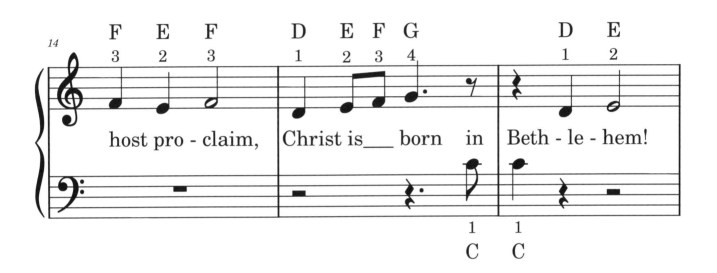

We Three Kings

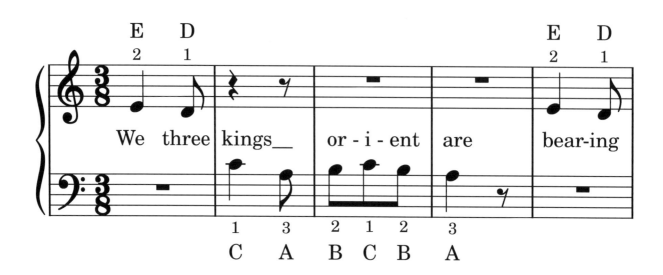

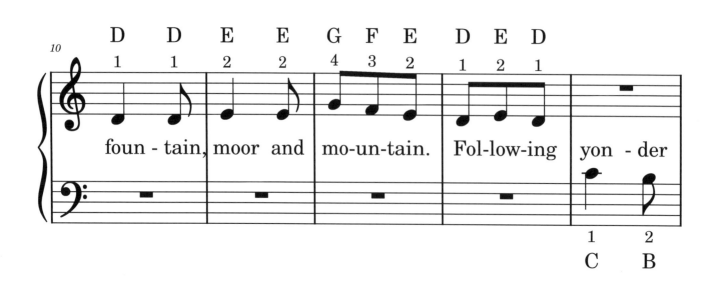

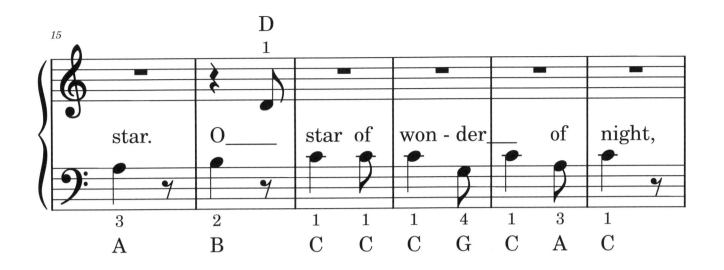

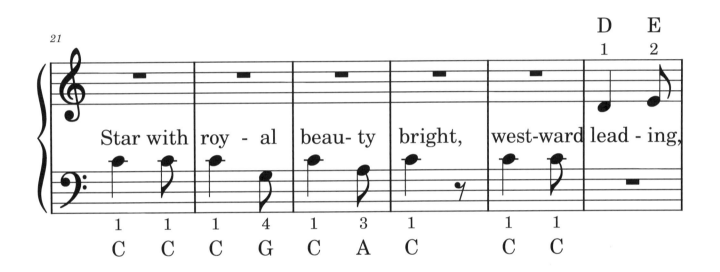

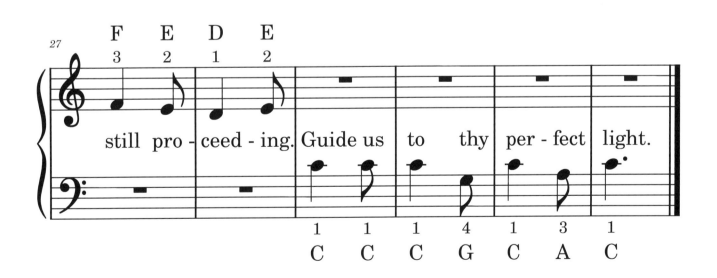

What Child is This (Greensleeves)

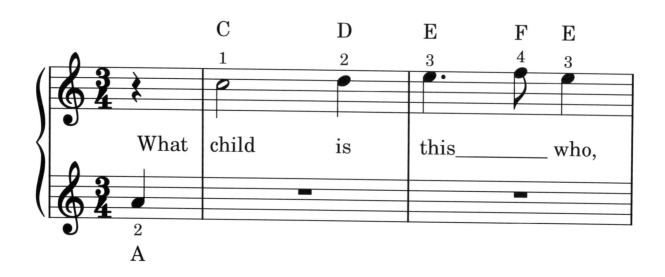

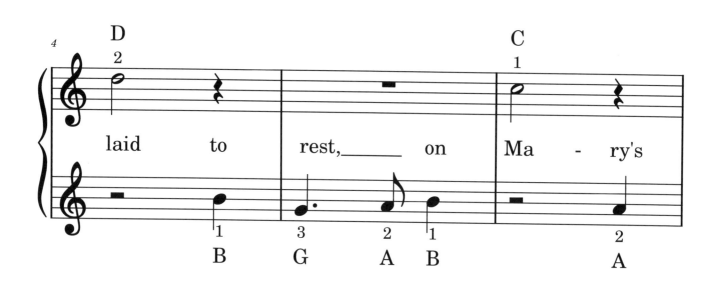

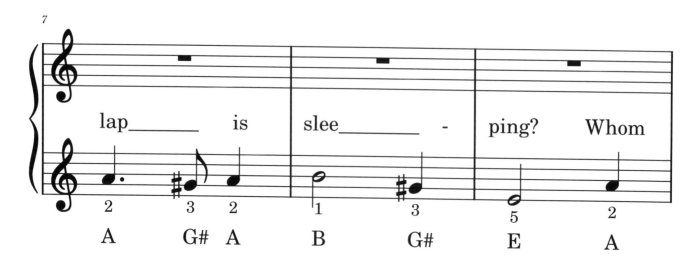

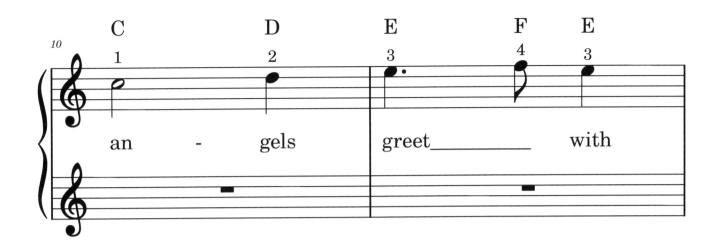

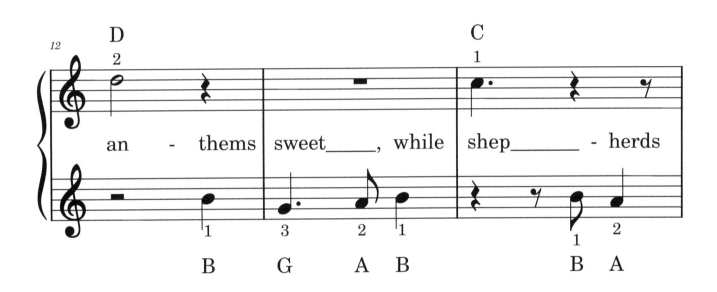

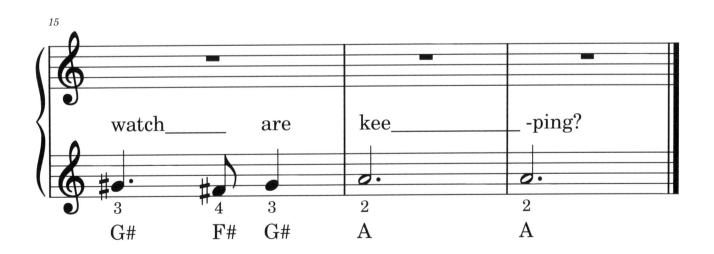

Ding Dong Merrily on High

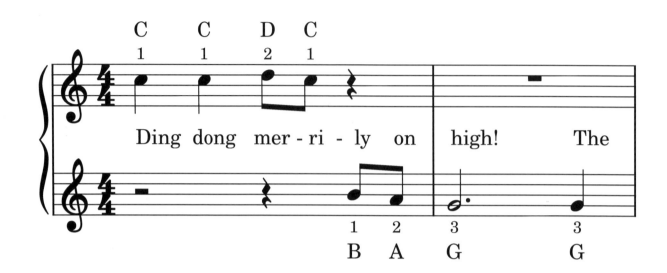

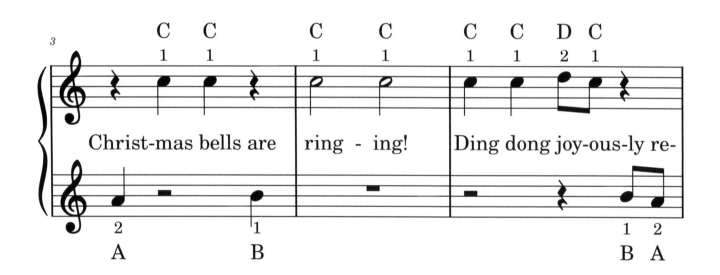

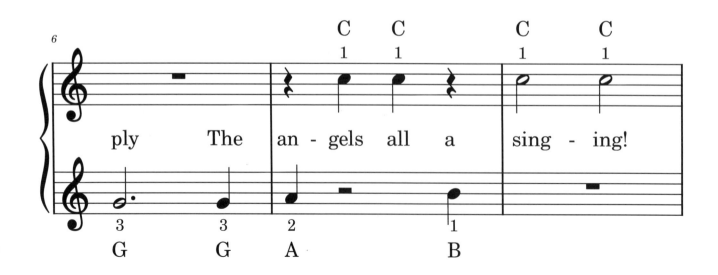

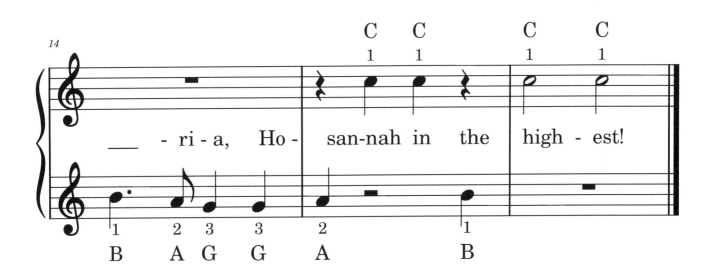

O Come, O Come, Emmanuel

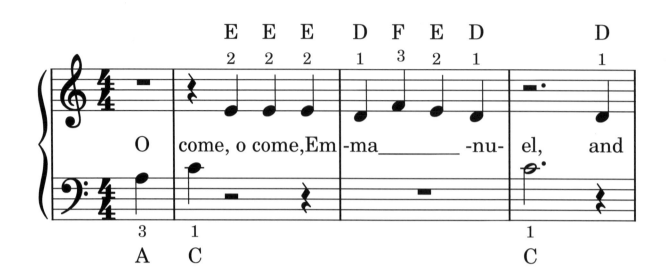

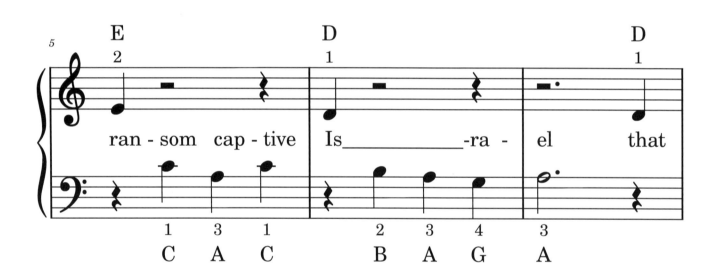

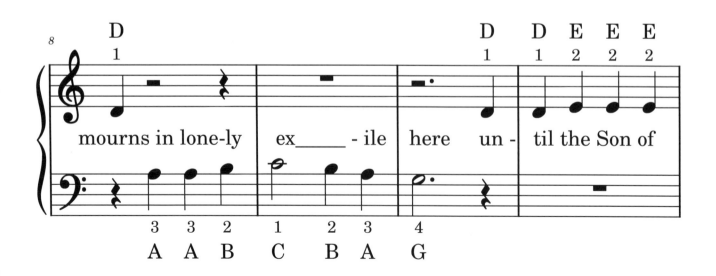

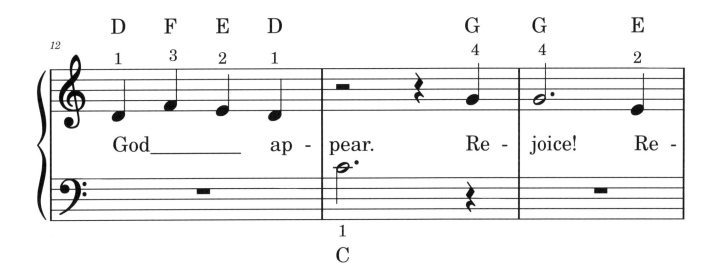

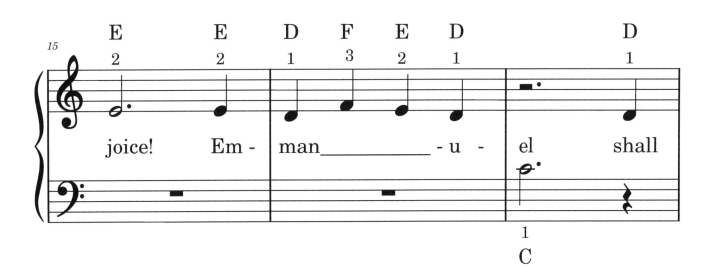

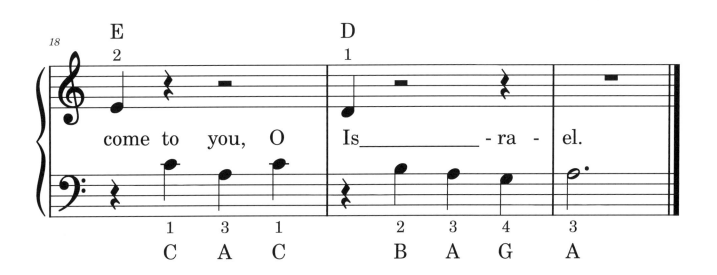

It Came Upon the Midnight Clear

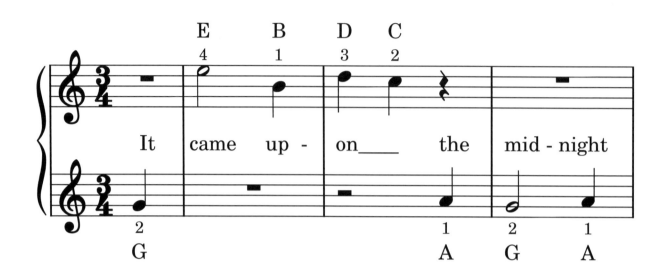

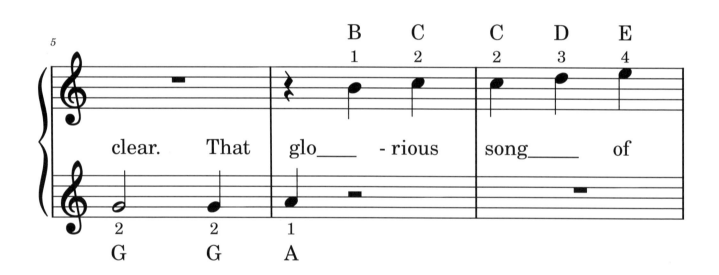

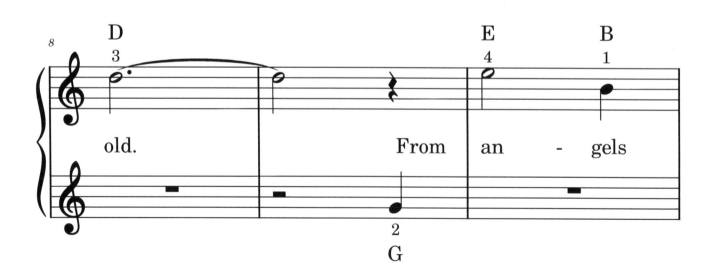

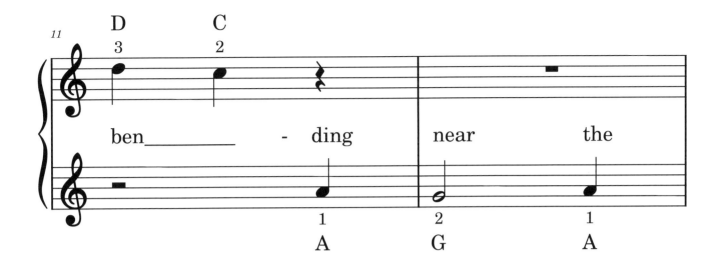

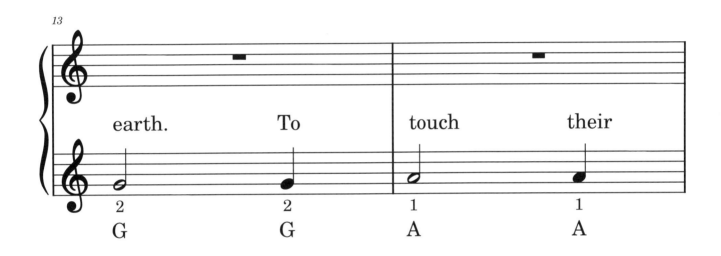

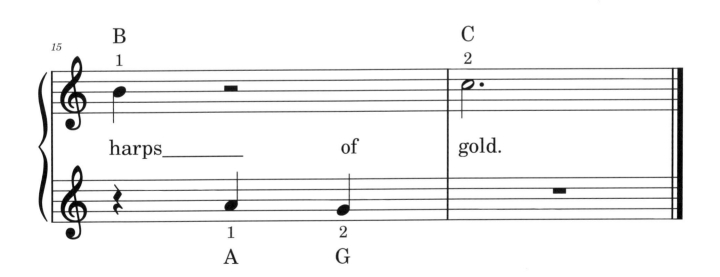

God Rest Ye Merry, Gentlemen

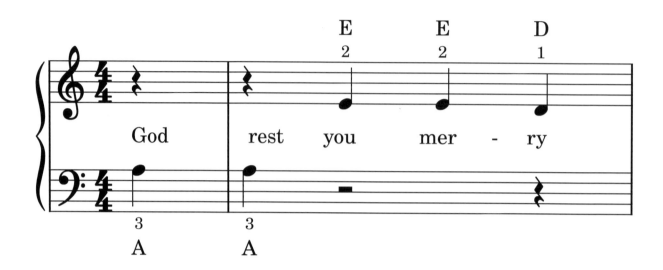

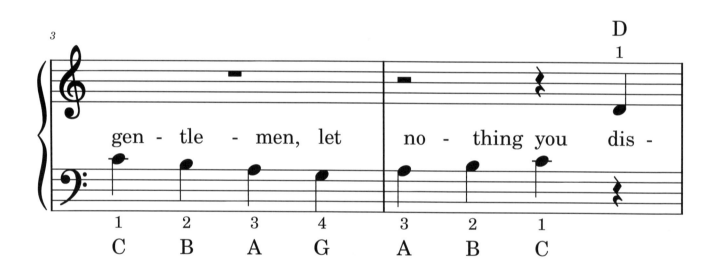

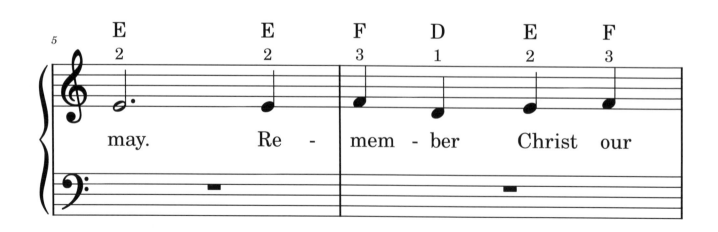

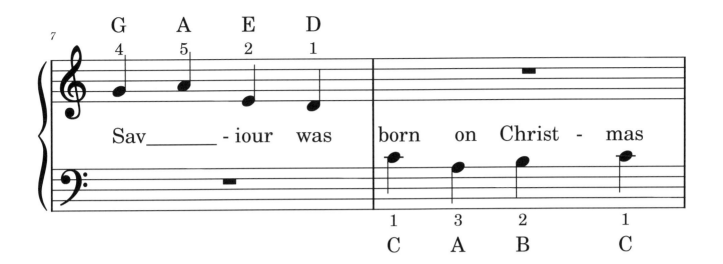

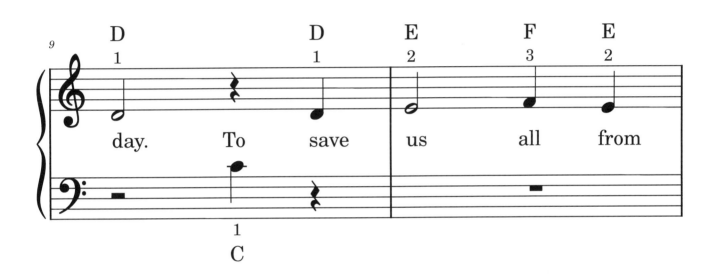

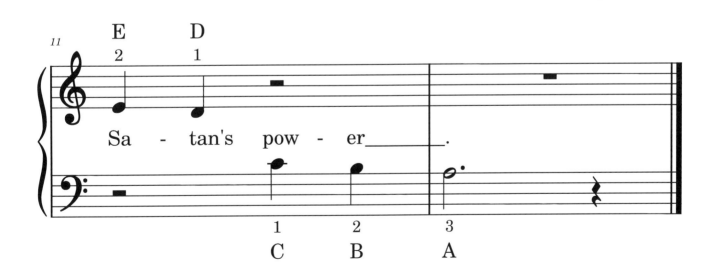

45

Go Tell It on the Mountain

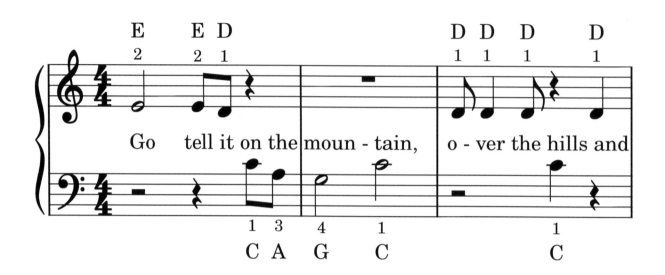

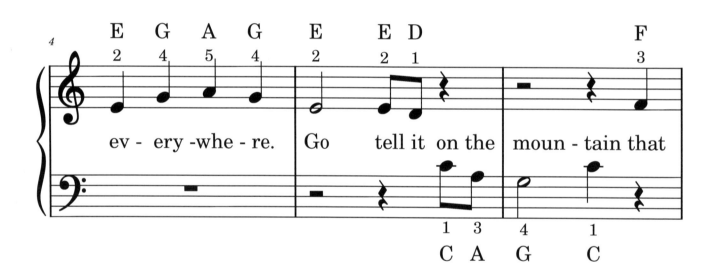

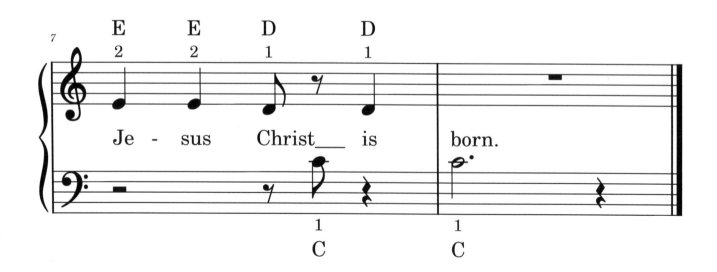

The Holly and the Ivy

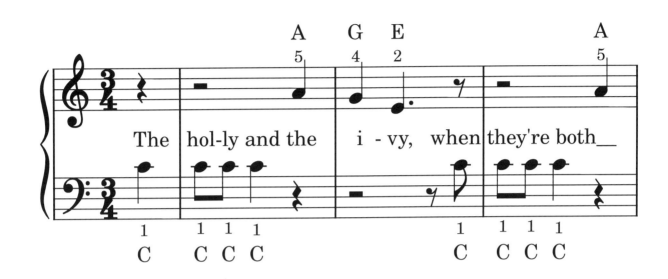

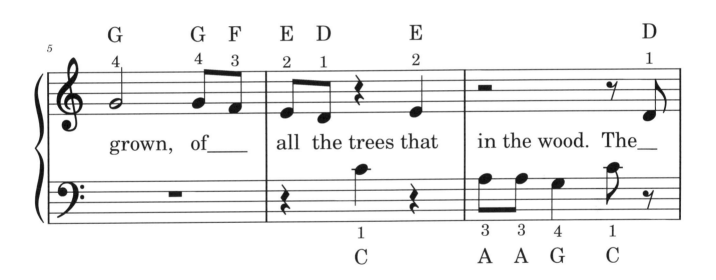

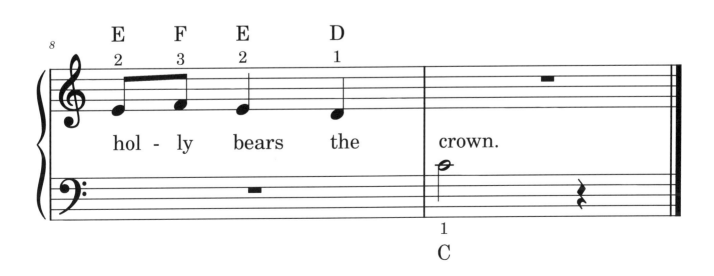

While Shepherds Watched Their Flocks

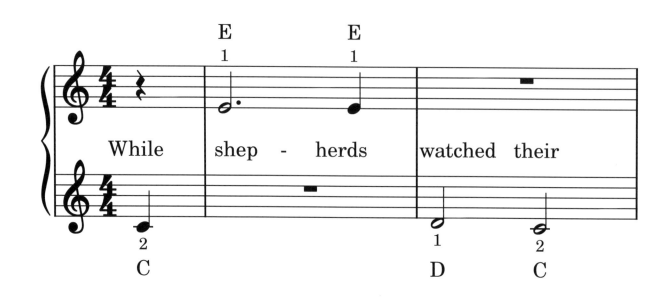

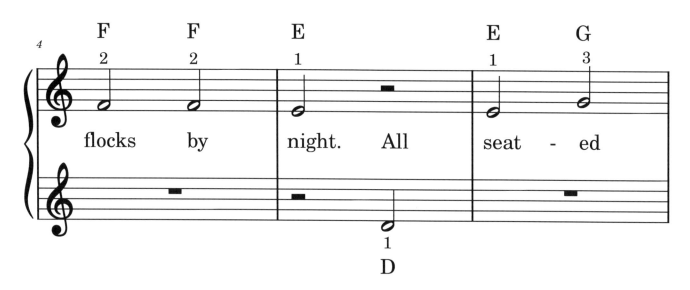

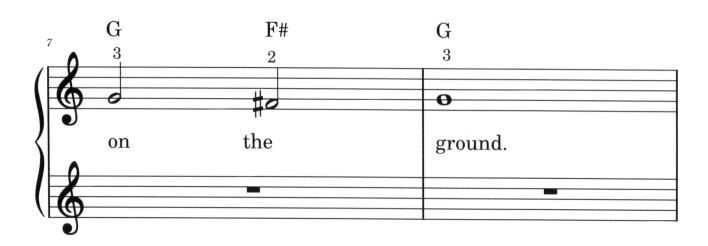

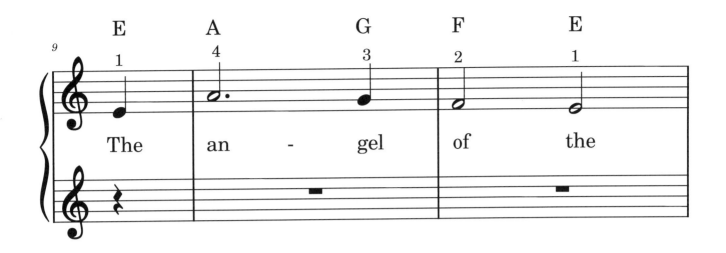

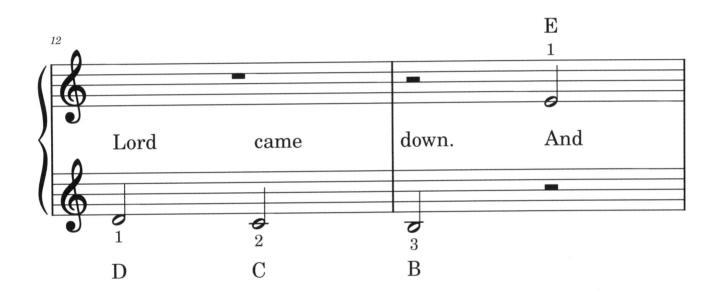

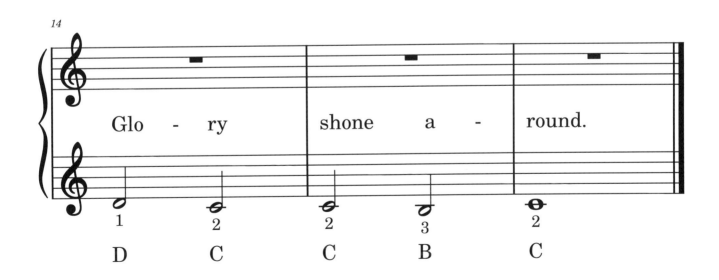

Good King Wenceslas

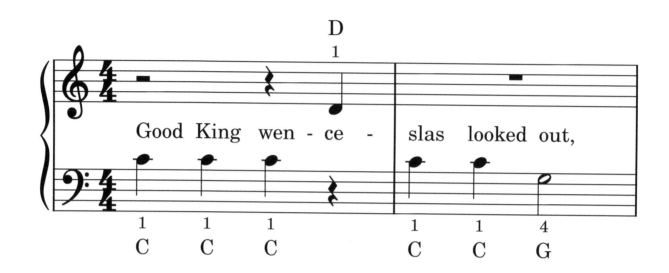

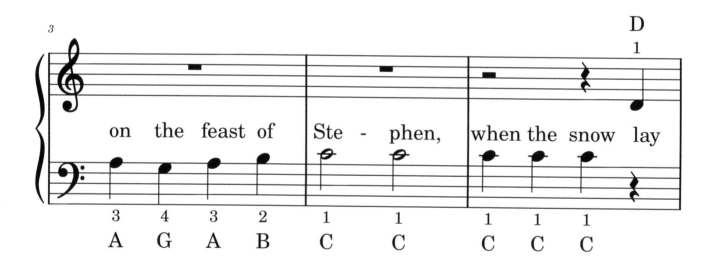

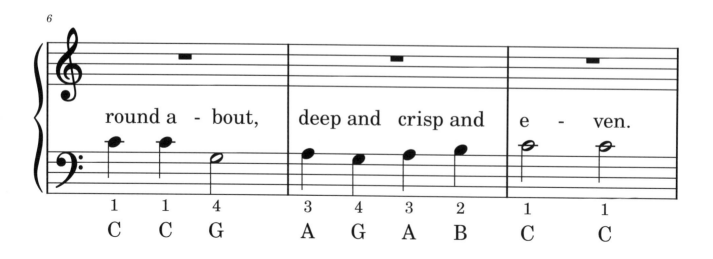

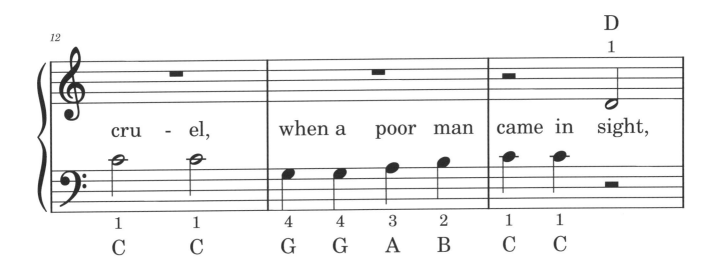

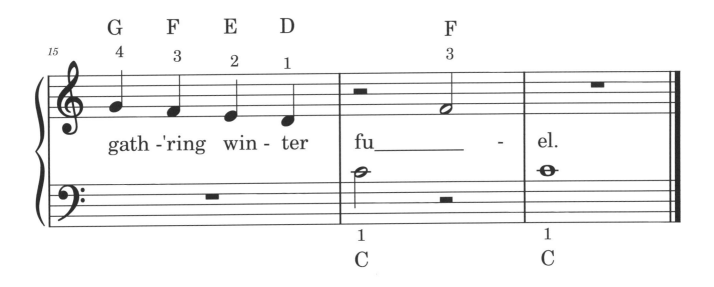

Away in a Manger

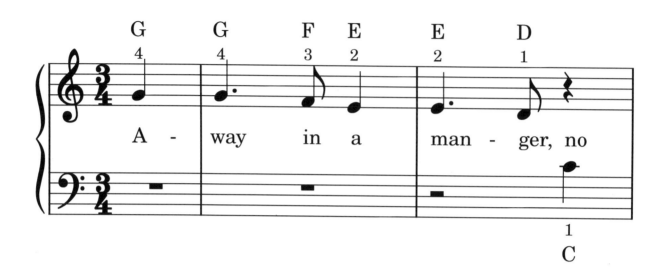

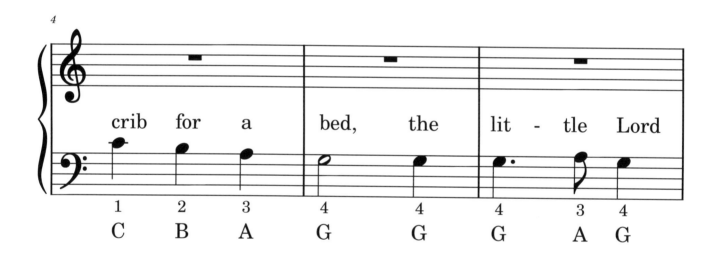

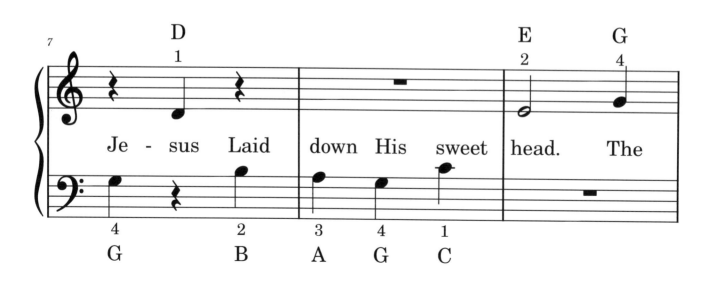

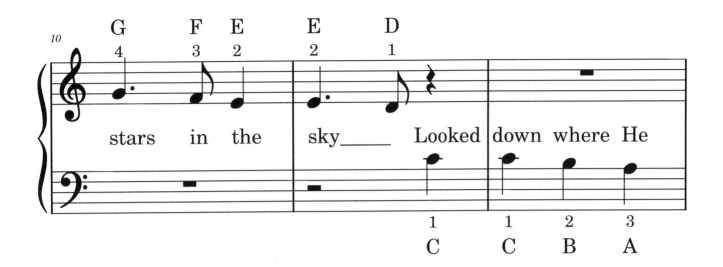

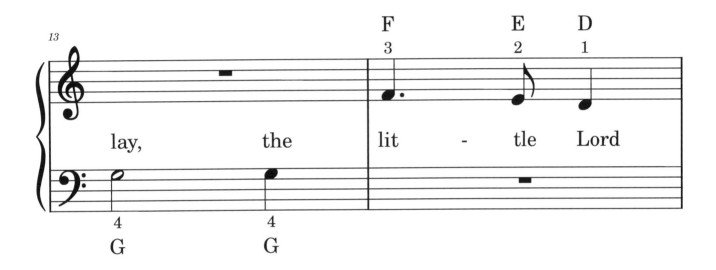

The Twelve Days of Christmas

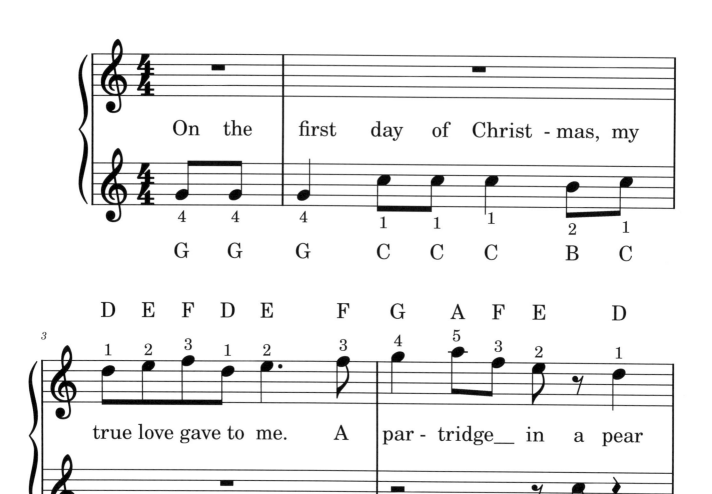

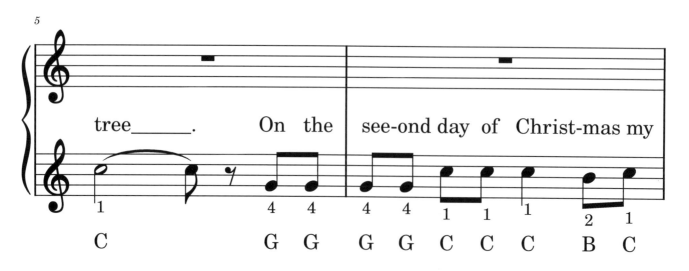

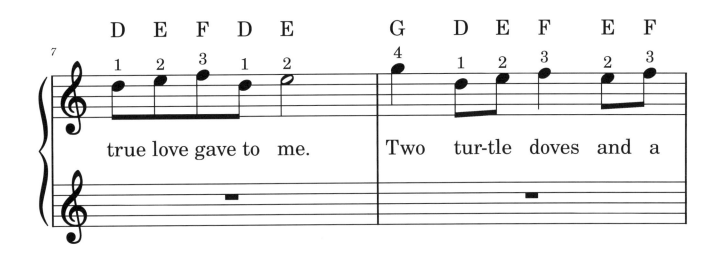

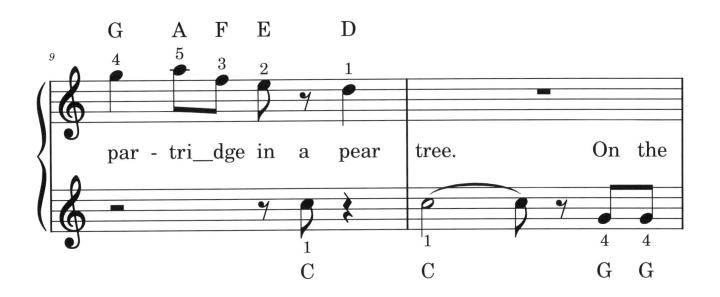

The Wassail Song

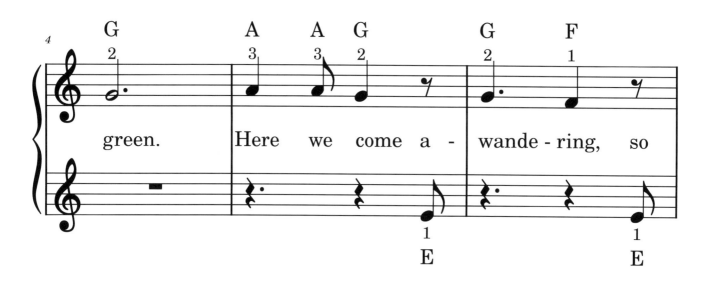

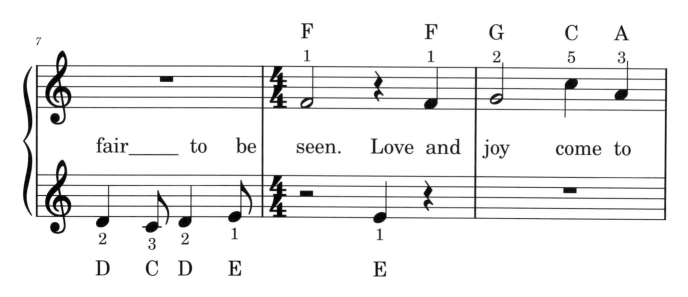

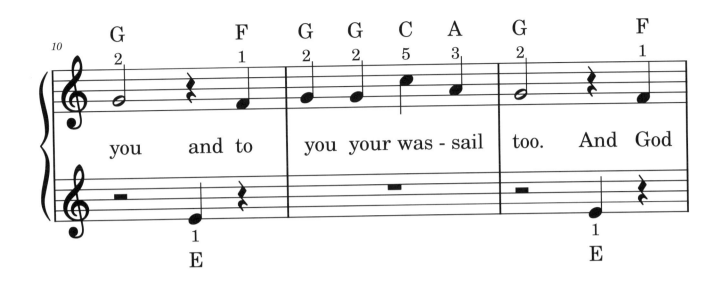

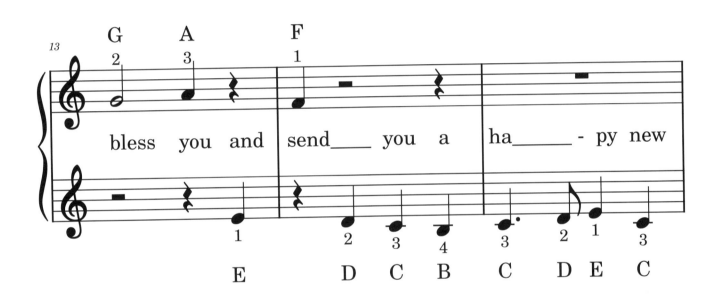

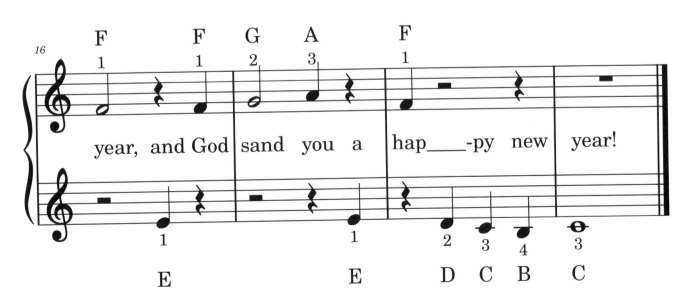

Bring a Torch, Jeanette, Isabella

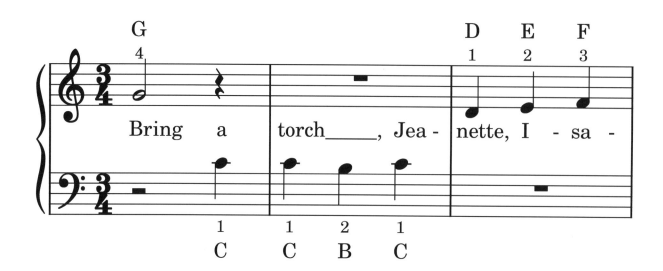

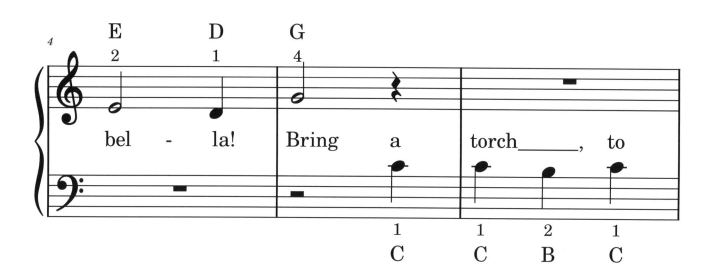

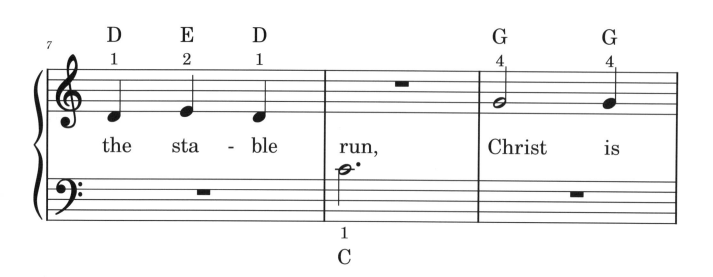

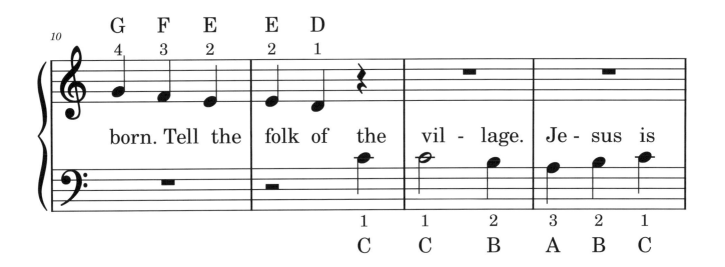

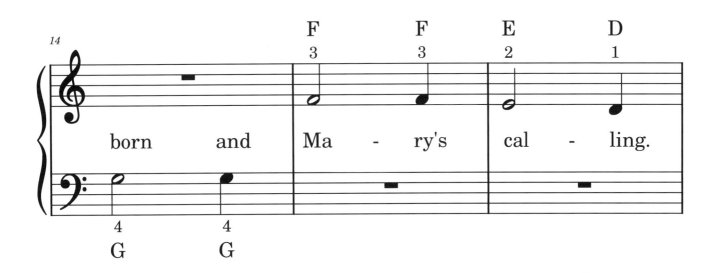

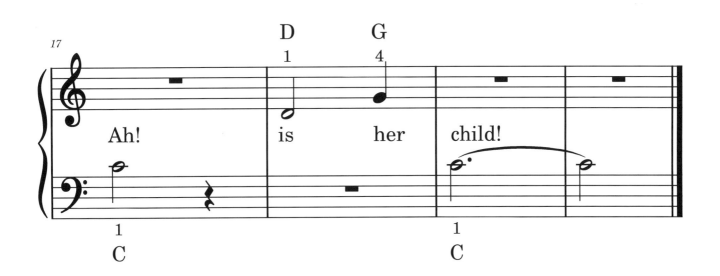

The Sussex Carol

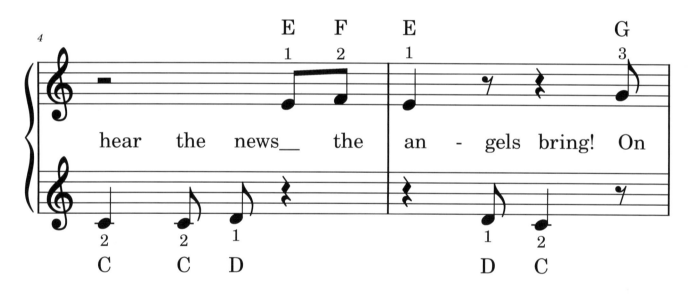

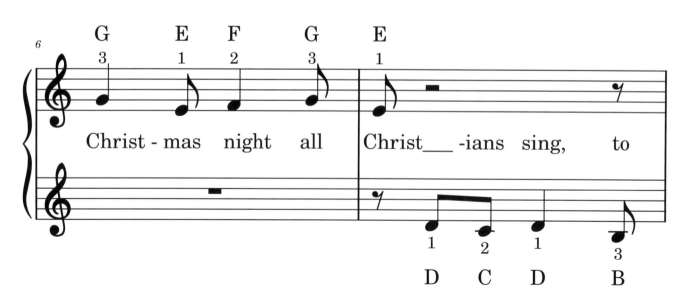

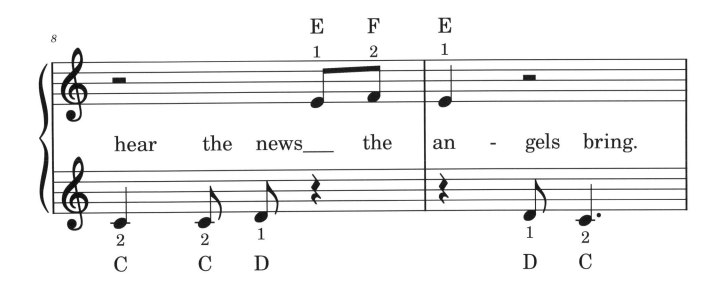

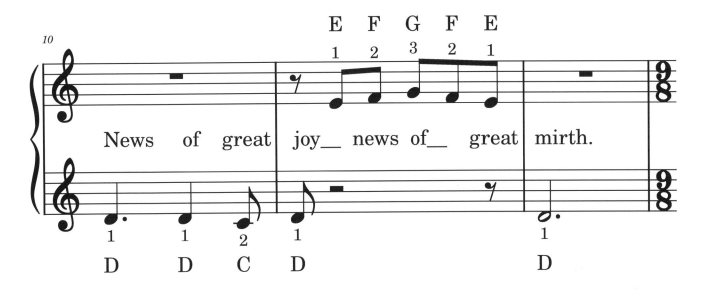

Coventry Carol

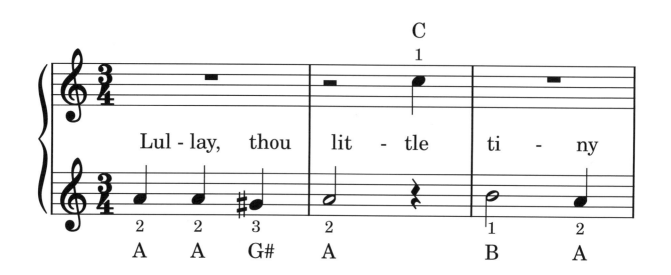

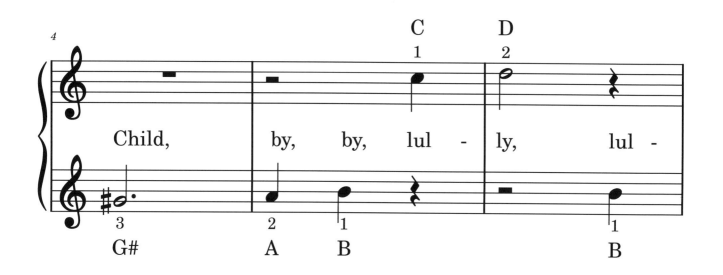

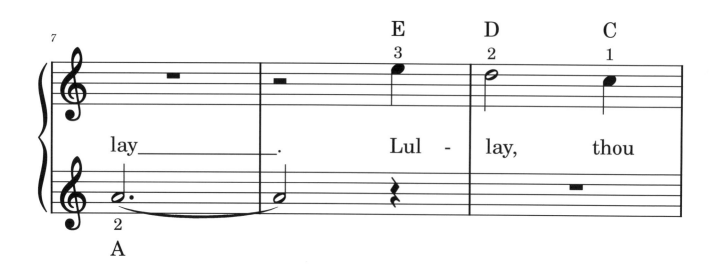

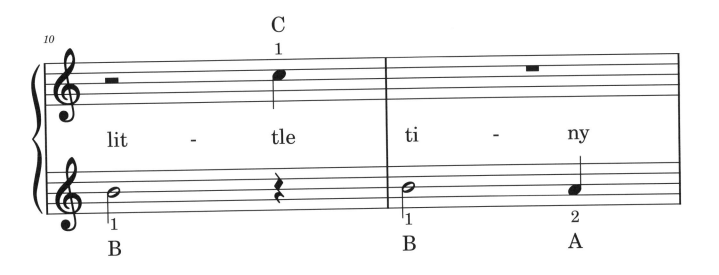

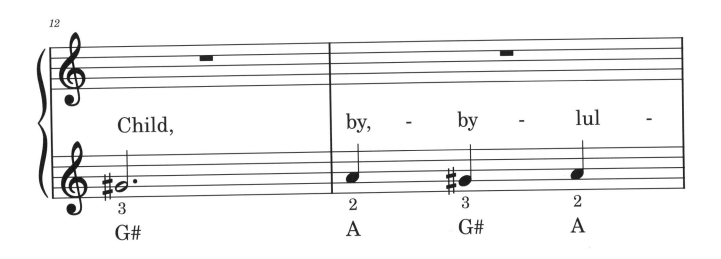

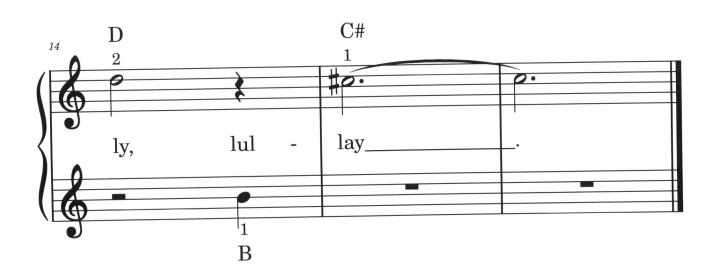

I Heard the Bells on Christmas Day

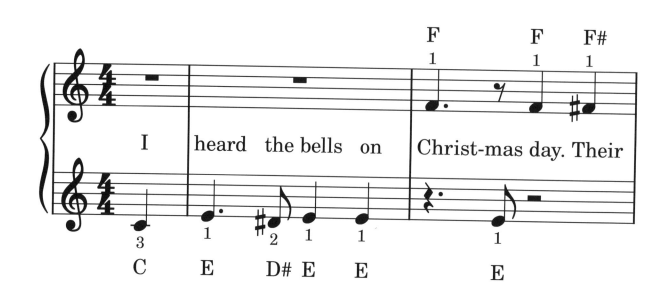

The Wexford Carol

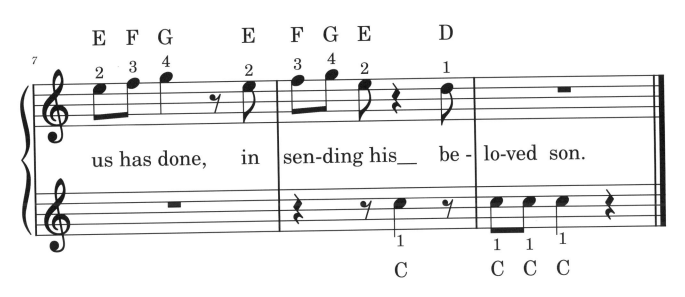

The Huron Carol

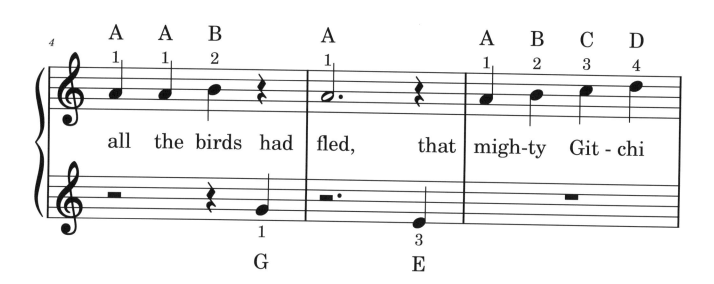

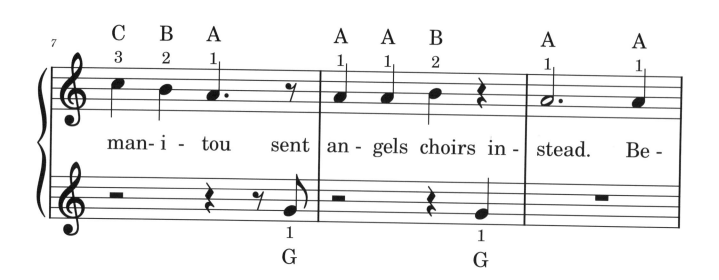

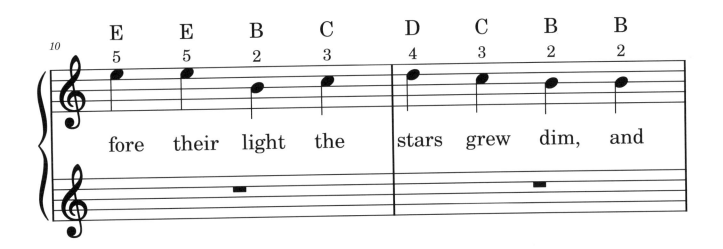

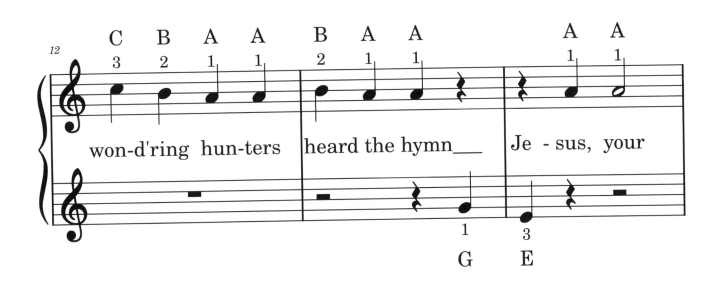

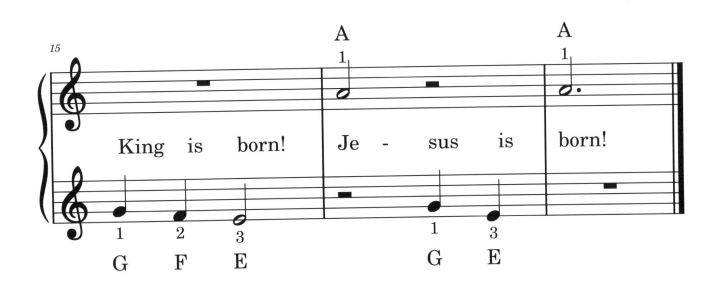

Wassail, Wassail All Over the Town

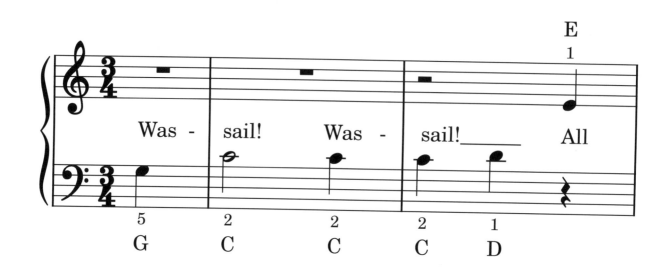

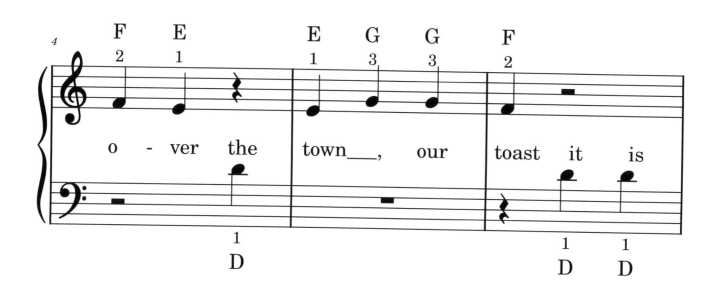

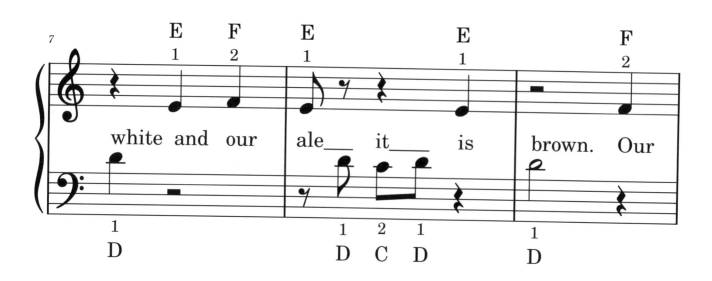

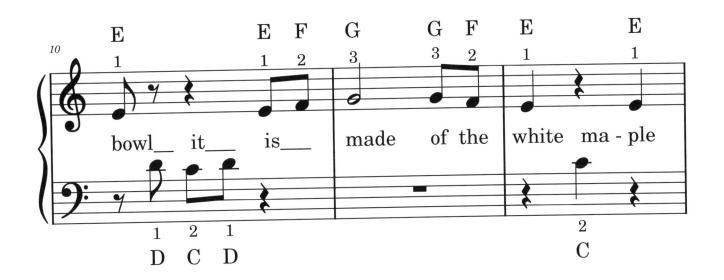

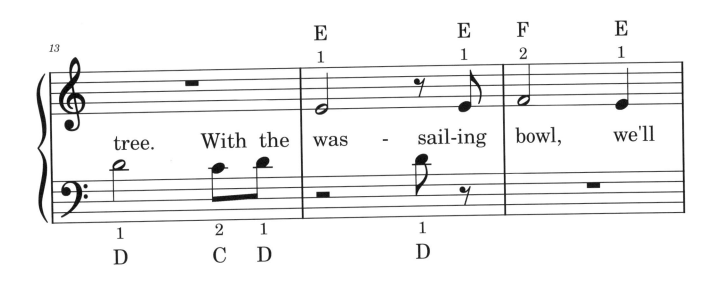

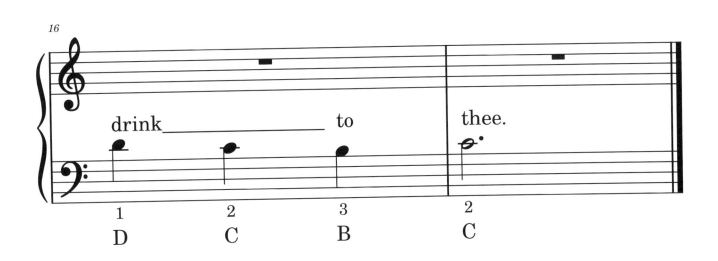

The Friendly Beasts

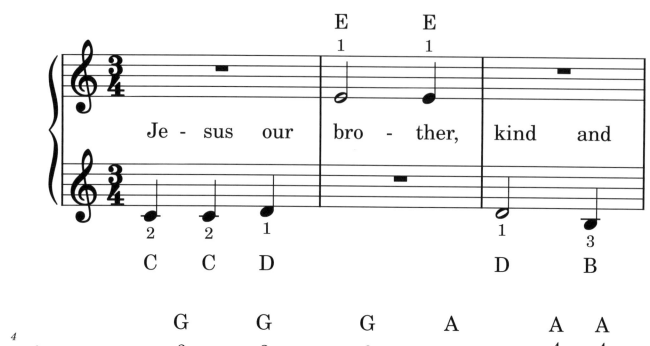

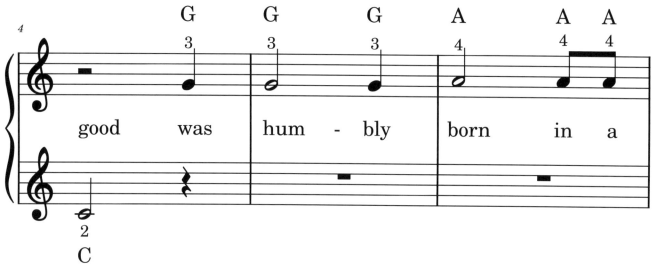

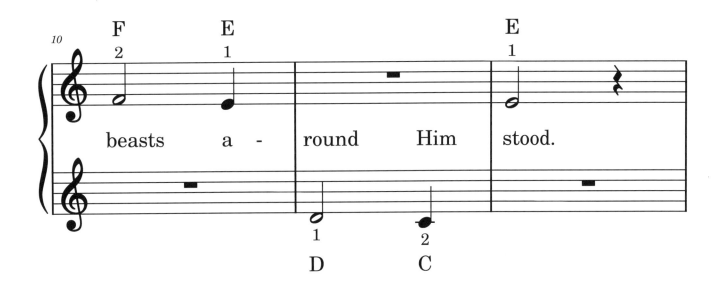

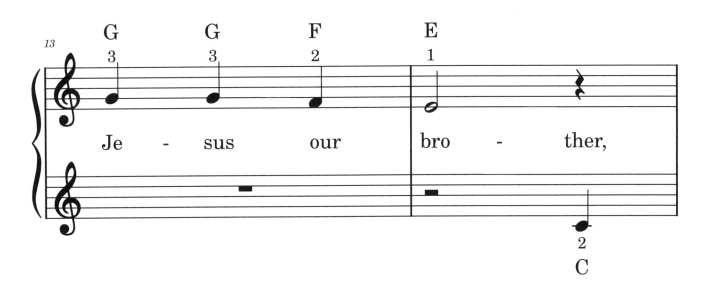

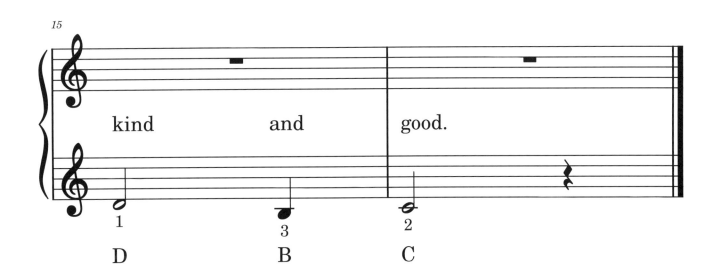

The Cherry Tree Carol

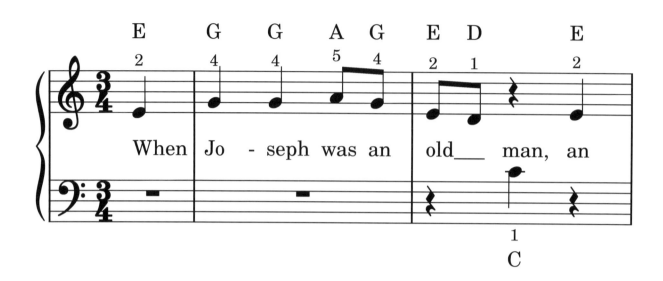

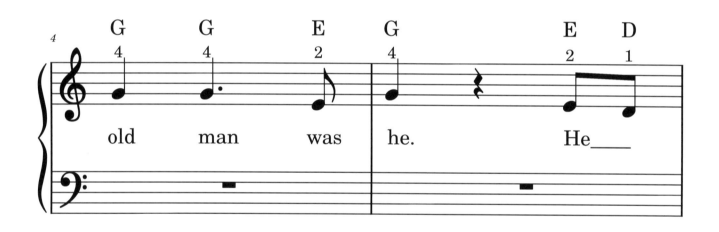

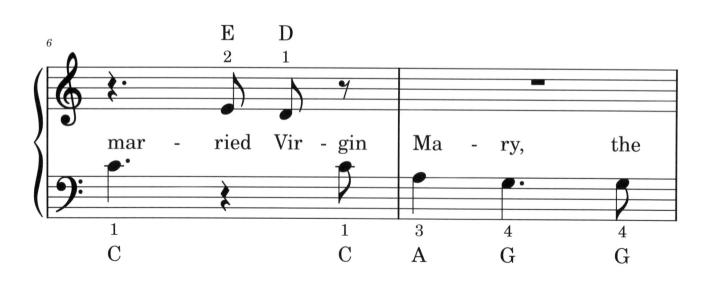

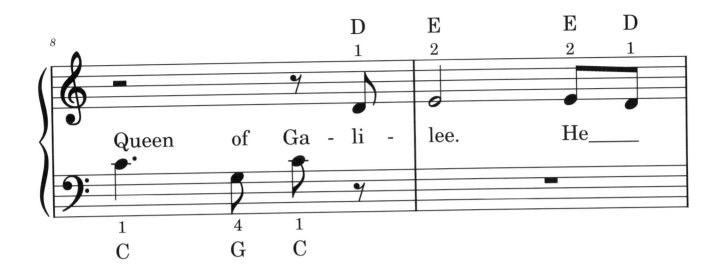

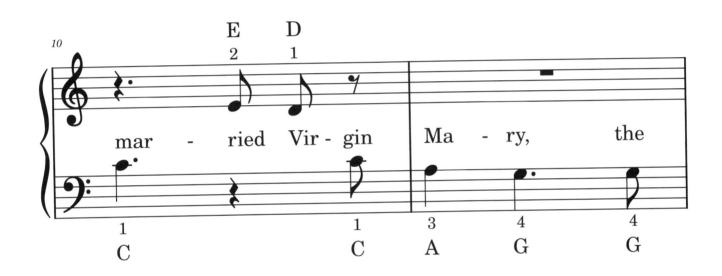

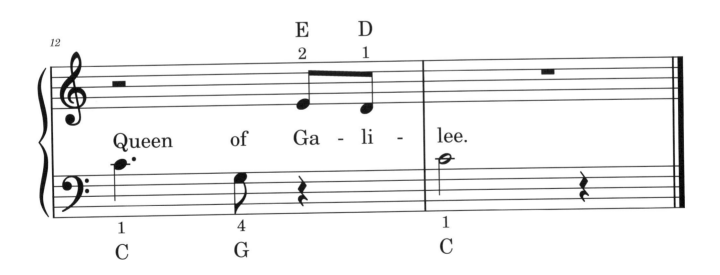

Lo, How a Rose E'er Blooming

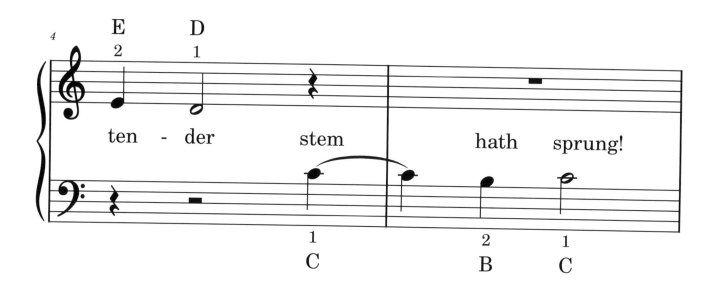

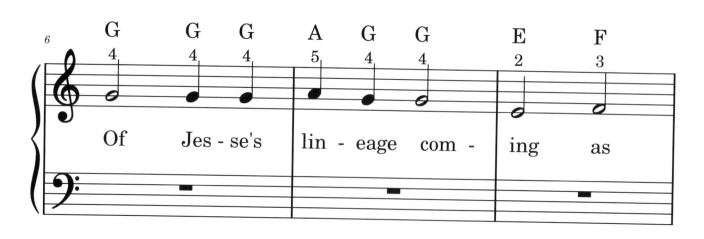

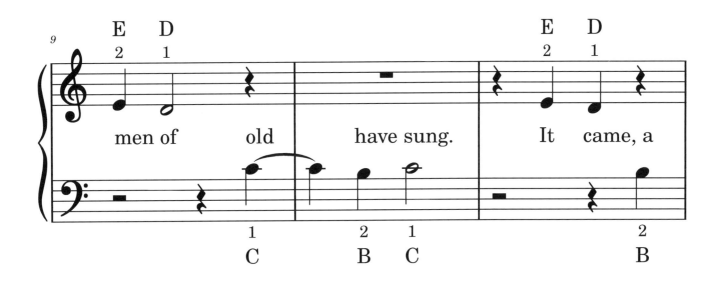

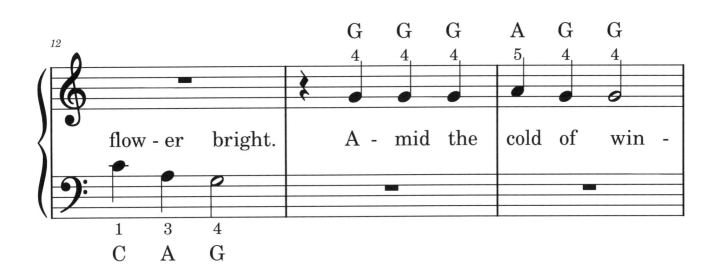

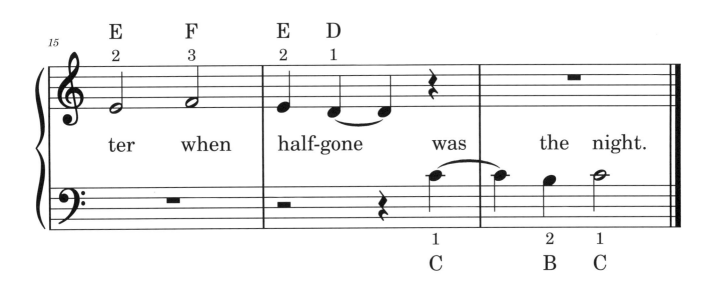

75

As Lately We Watched

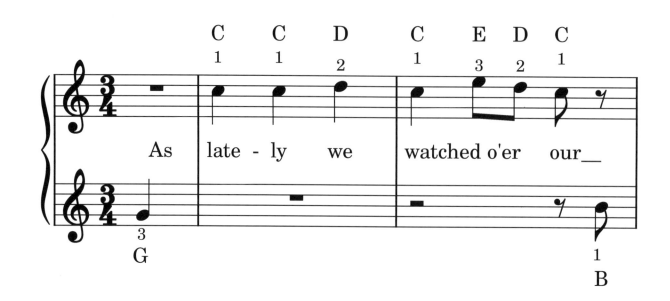

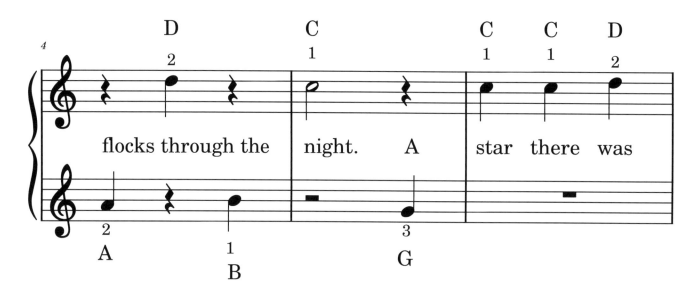

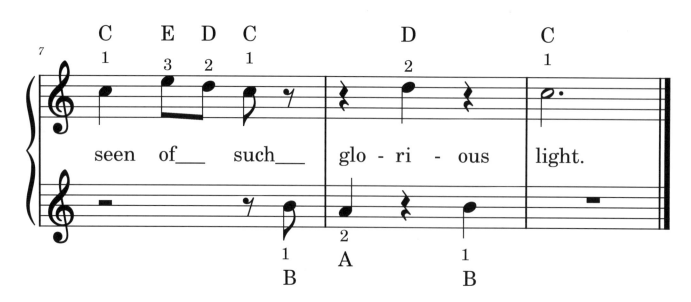

In the Bleak Midwinter

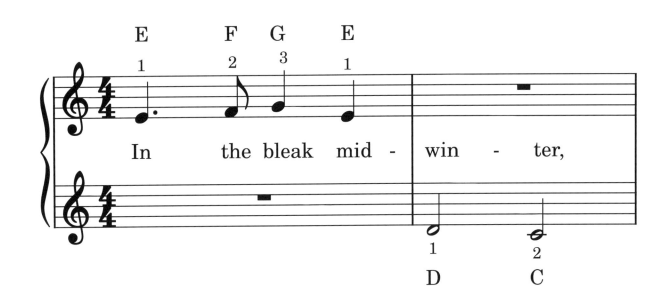

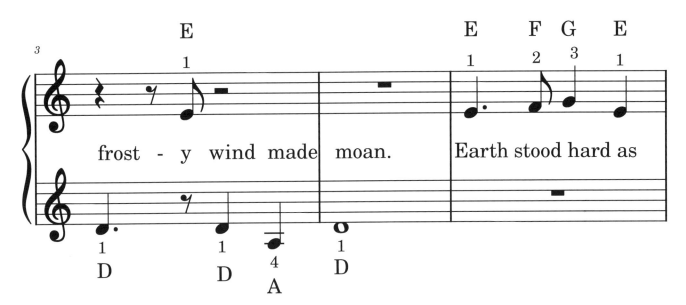

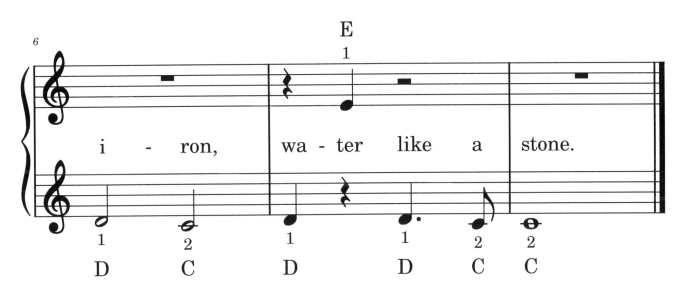

The Seven Joys of Mary

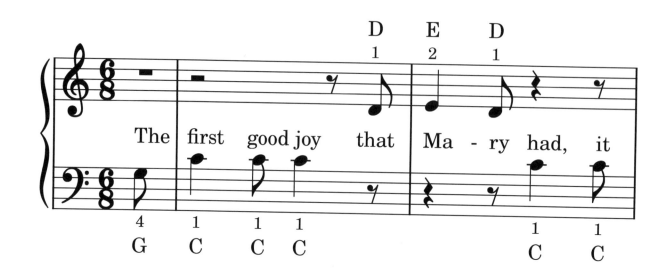

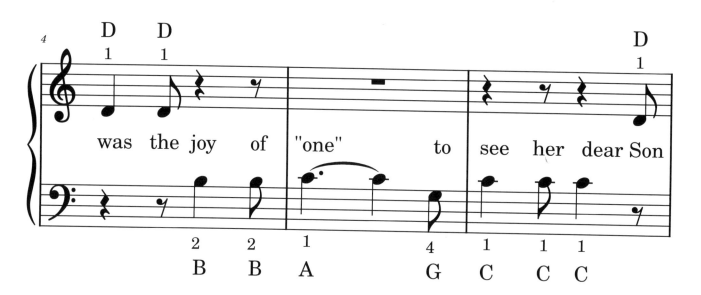

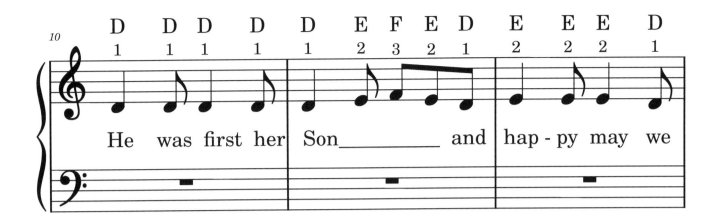

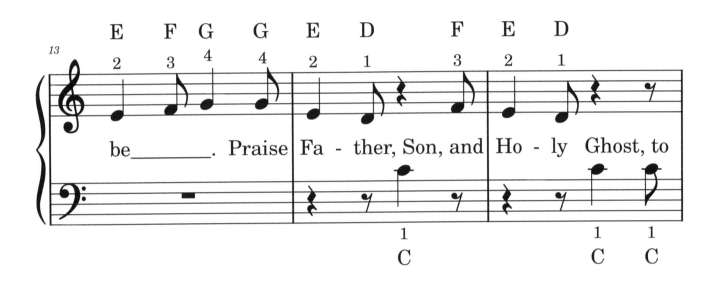

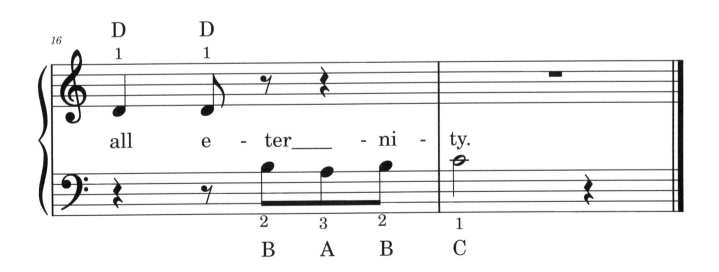

The Carol of the Birds

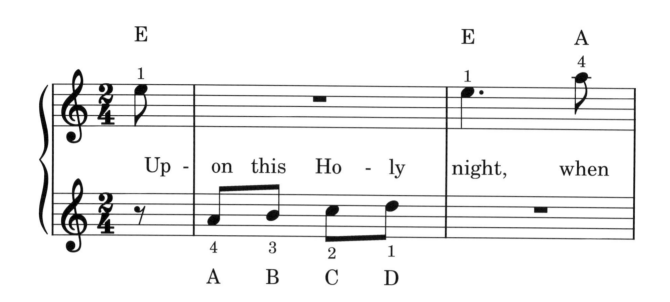

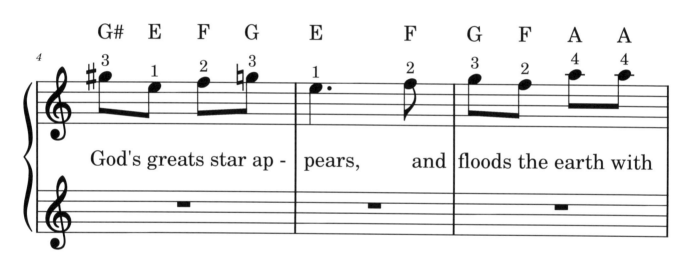

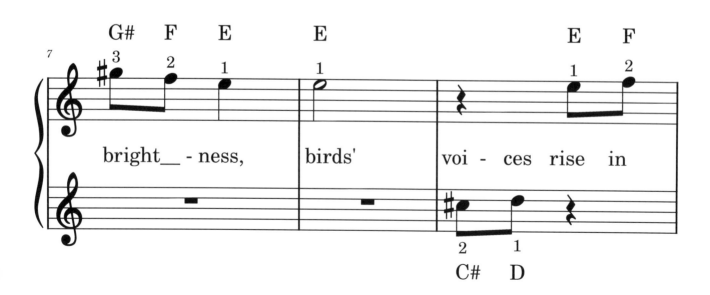

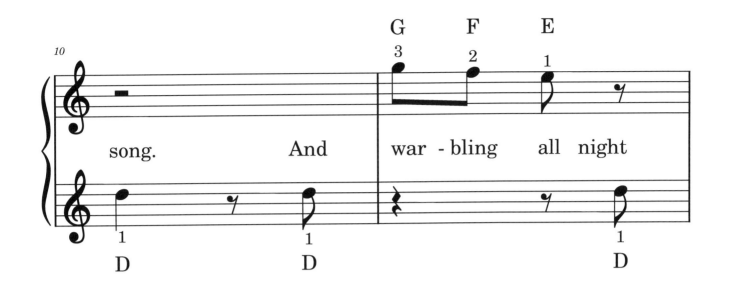

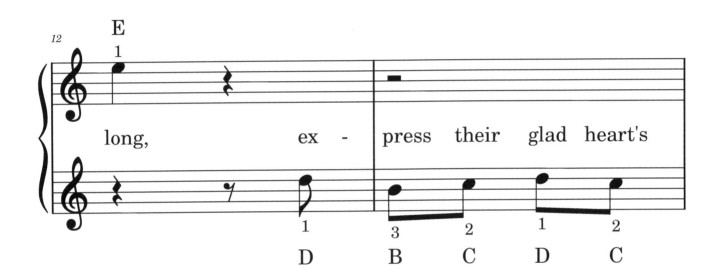

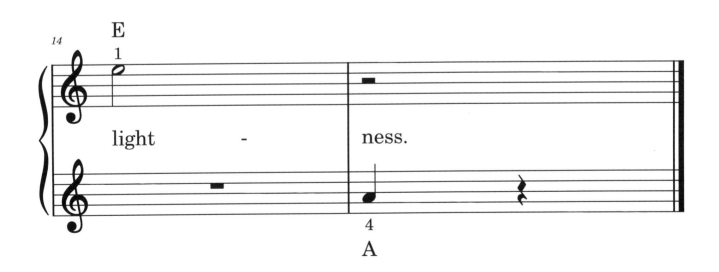

O Come, Little Children

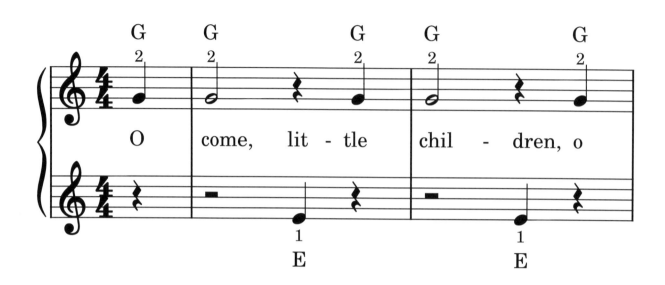

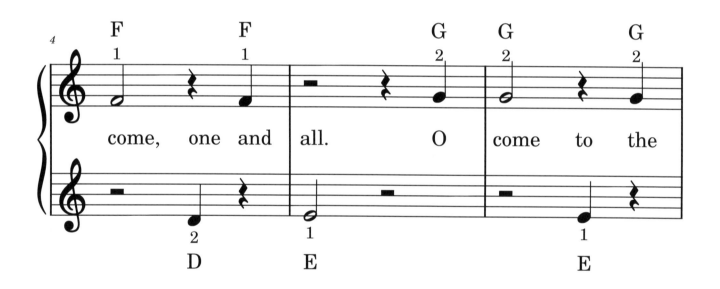

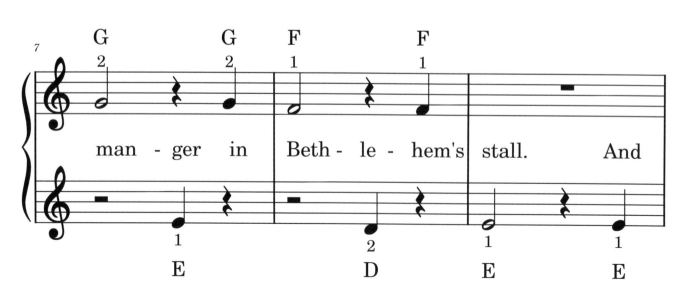

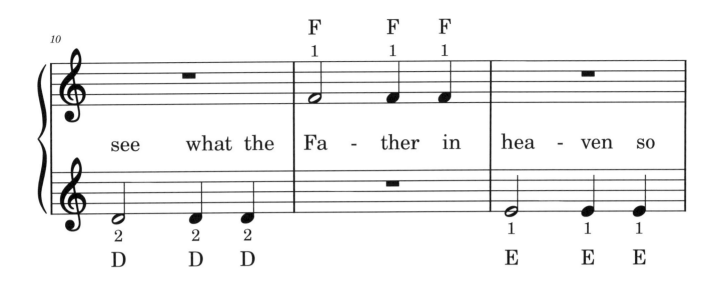

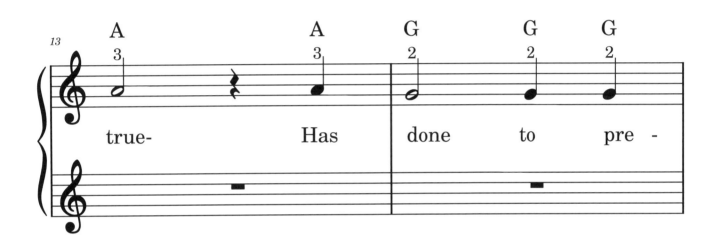

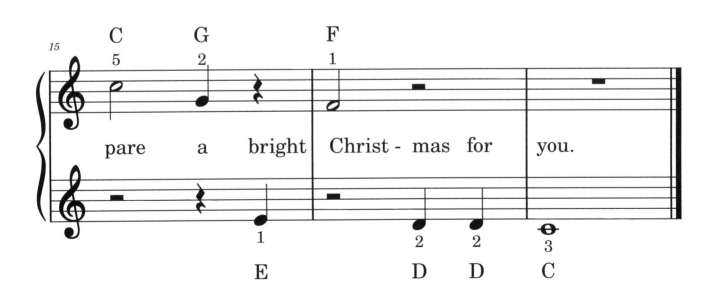

The New Year Carol

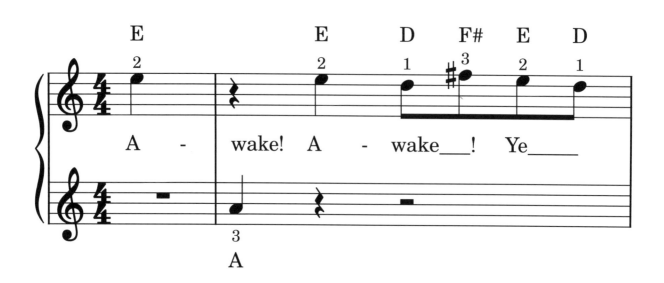

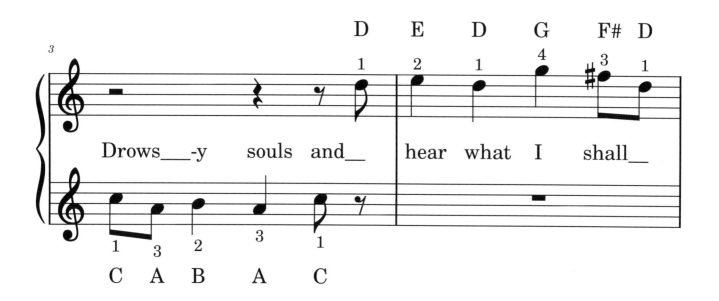

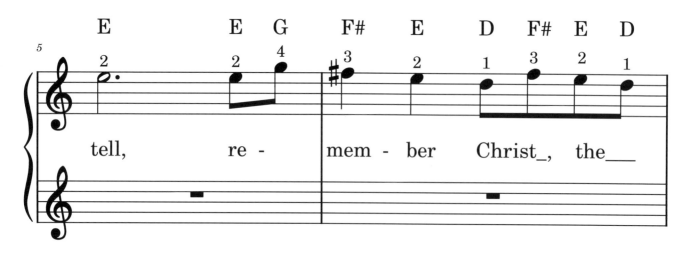

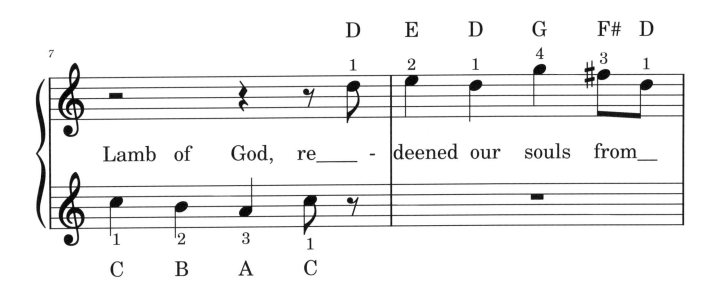

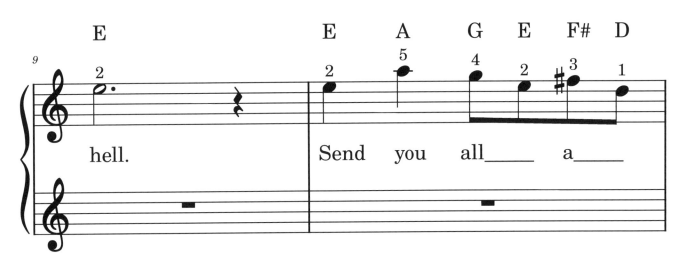

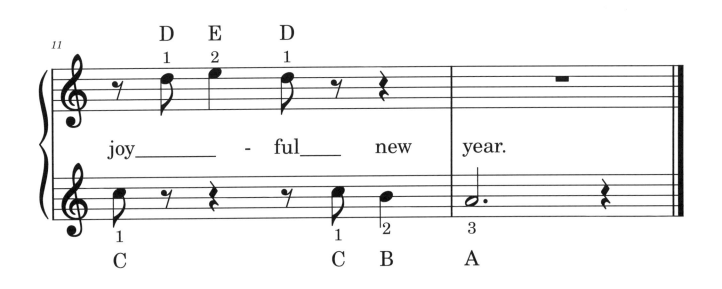

Once in Royal David's City

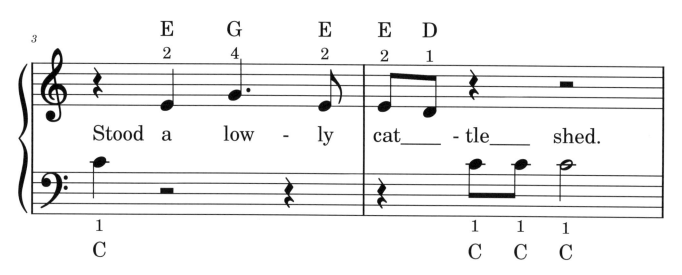

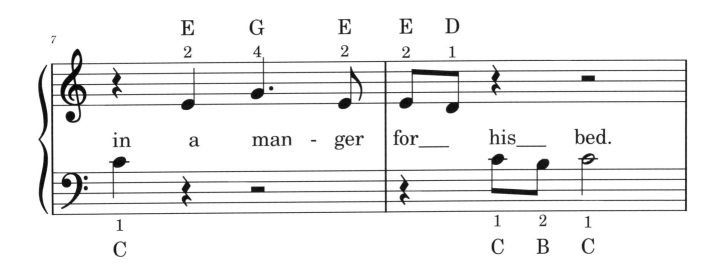

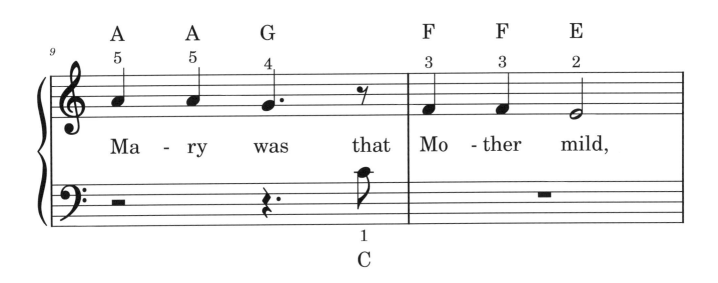

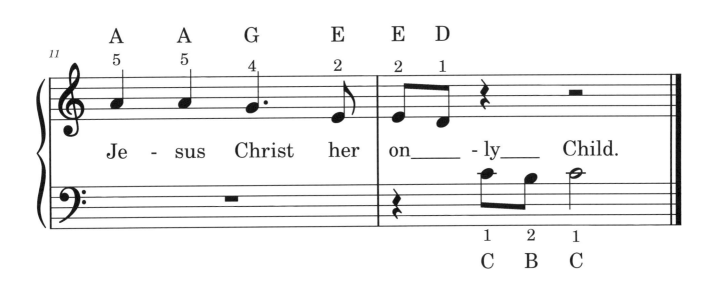

Ich steh' an deiner Krippen hier

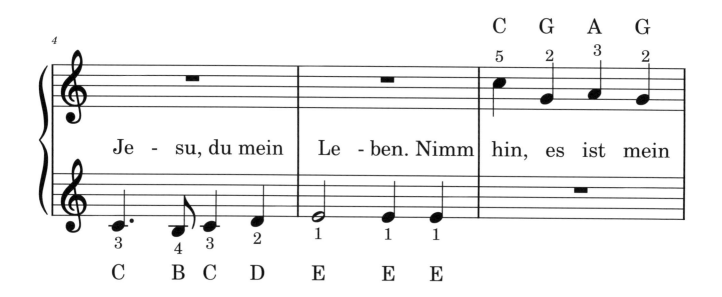

Alle Jahre wieder

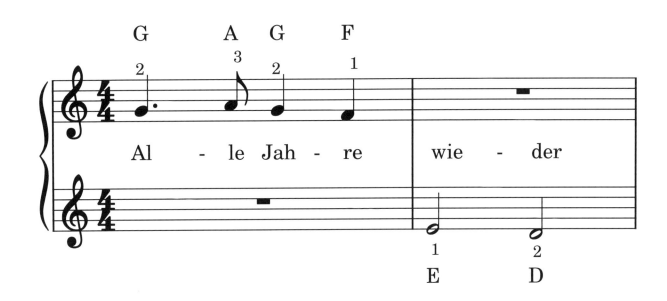

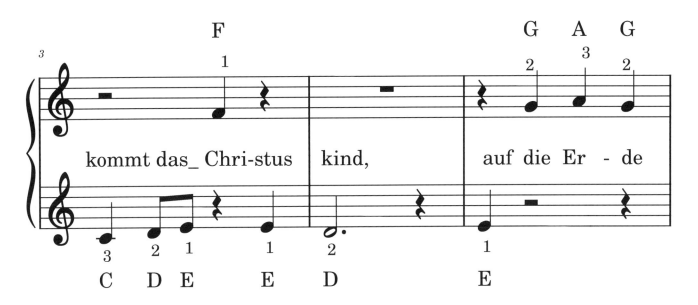

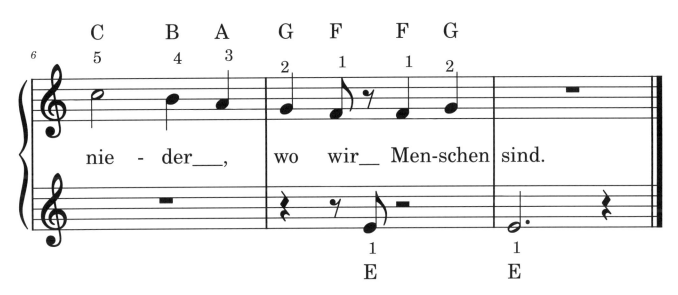

Sing We Now Of Christmas

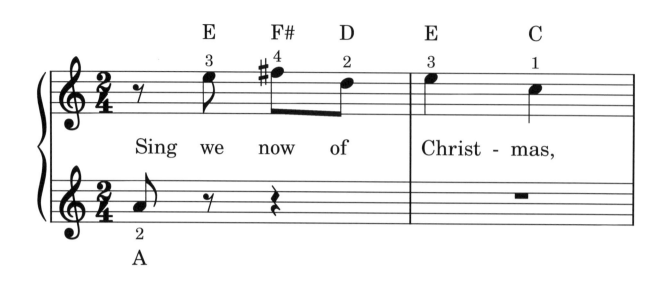

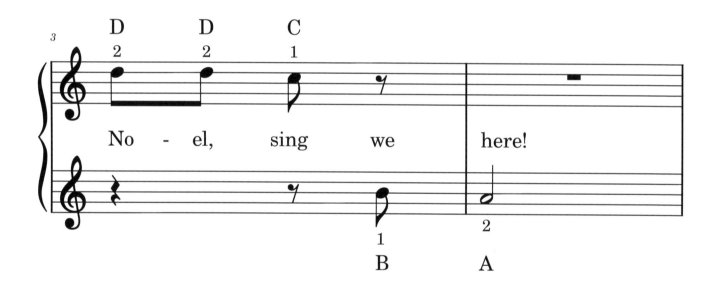

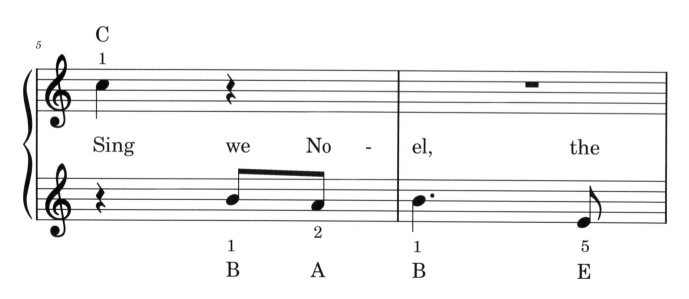

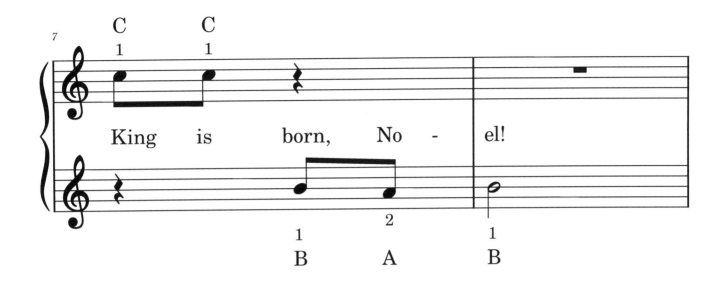

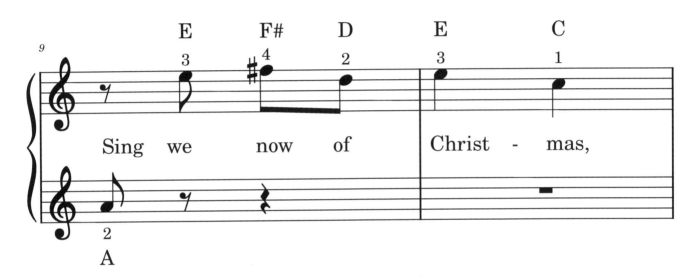

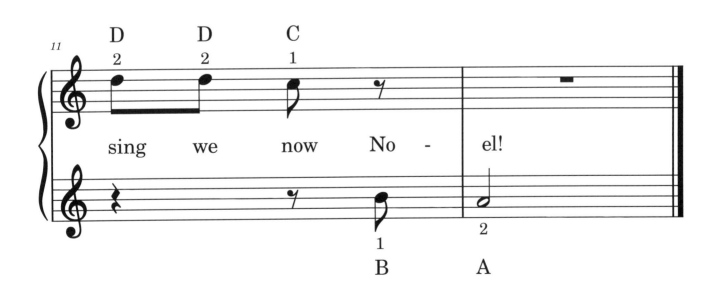

Come, Thou Long-Expected Jesus

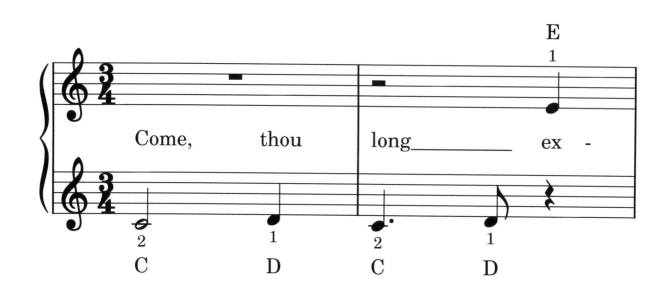

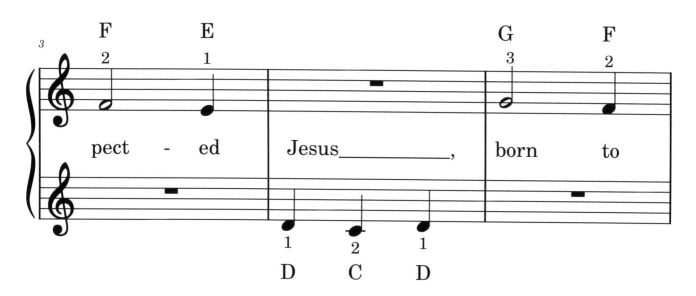

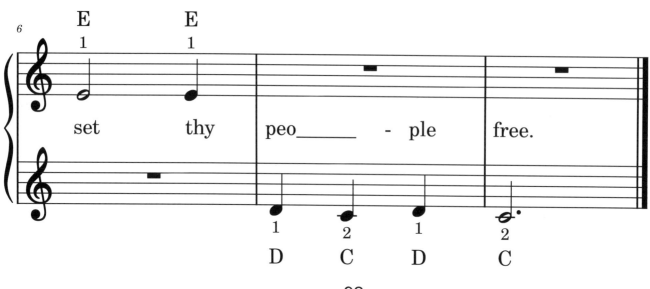

The Babe of Bethlehem

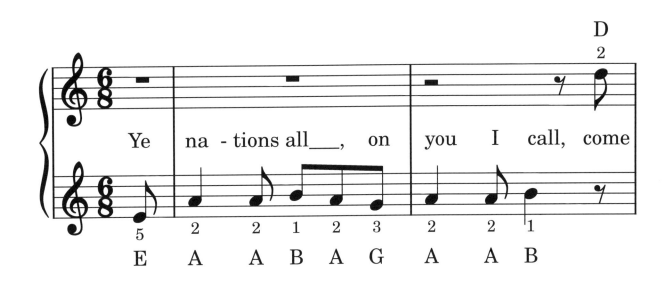

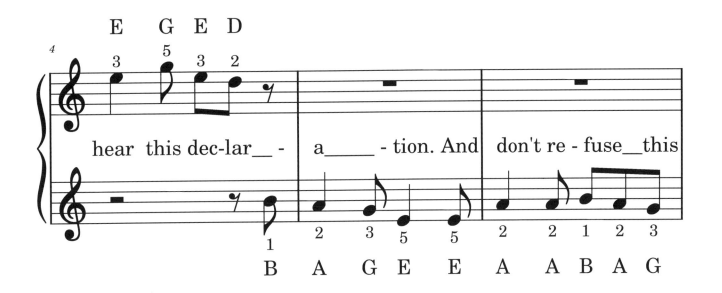

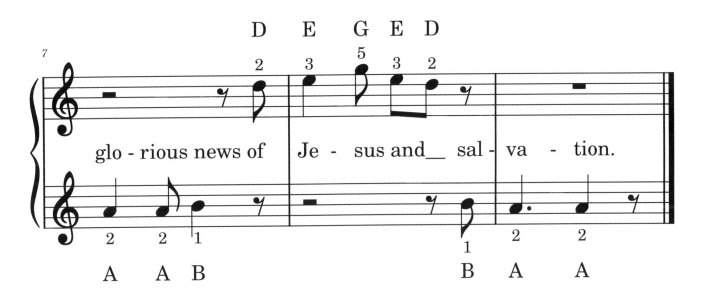

Up on the Housetop

Made in the USA
Middletown, DE
03 December 2024

66021284R00053